THE LOVER

TEA PARTY

THE BASEMENT

Two plays and a film script

by

Harold Pinter

Grove Press, Inc.
New York

Eighth Printing 1977
ISBN: 0-394-17263-9
Grove Press ISBN: 0-8021-4121-8
Library of Congress Catalog Card Number:
67-27884

Manufactured in the United States of America

Distributed by Random House, Inc., New York

GROVE PRESS, INC., 196 West Houston Street,
New York, N.Y. 10014

HC 13

THE LOVER

THE LOVER was first presented by Associated-Rediffusion Television, London, March 28th, 1963, with the following cast:

RICHARD	Alan Badel
SARAH	Vivien Merchant
JOHN	Michael Forrest

Directed by Joan Kemp-Welch

The play was first presented on the stage by Michael Codron and David Hall at the Arts Theatre, September 18th, 1963, with the following cast:

RICHARD	Scott Forbes
SARAH	Vivien Merchant
JOHN	Michael Forrest

Directed by Harold Pinter

Assisted by Guy Vaesen

Summer. A detached house near Windsor

The stage consists of two areas. Living-room right, with small hall and front door up centre. Bedroom and balcony, on a level, left. There is a short flight of stairs to bedroom door. Kitchen off right. A table with a long velvet cover stands against the left wall of the living-room, centre stage. In the small hall there is a cupboard. The furnishings are tasteful, comfortable.

SARAH *is emptying and dusting ashtrays in the living-room. It is morning. She wears a crisp, demure dress.* RICHARD *comes into the bedroom from bathroom, off left, collects his briefcase from hall cupboard, goes to* SARAH, *kisses her on the cheek. He looks at her for a moment smiling. She smiles.*

RICHARD (*amiably*). Is your lover coming today?
SARAH. Mmnn.
RICHARD. What time?
SARAH. Three.
RICHARD. Will you be going out . . . or staying in?
SARAH. Oh . . . I think we'll stay in.
RICHARD. I thought you wanted to go to that exhibition.
SARAH. I did, yes . . . but I think I'd prefer to stay in with him today.
RICHARD. Mmn-hmmn. Well, I must be off.

He goes to the hall and puts on his bowler hat.

RICHARD. Will he be staying long do you think?
SARAH. Mmmnnn . . .
RICHARD. About . . . six, then.
SARAH. Yes.
RICHARD. Have a pleasant afternoon.
SARAH. Mmnn.
RICHARD. Bye-bye.
SARAH. Bye.

He opens the front door and goes out. She continues dusting.
The lights fade.
Fade up. Early evening. SARAH *comes into room from kitchen.*
She wears the same dress, but is now wearing a pair of very
high-heeled shoes. She pours a drink and sits on chaise longue
with magazine. There are six chimes of the clock. RICHARD
comes in the front door. He wears a sober suit, as in the
morning. He puts his briefcase down in the hall and goes into
the room. She smiles at him and pours him a whisky.

Hullo.

RICHARD. Hullo.

He kisses her on the cheek. Takes glass, hands her the evening
paper and sits down left. She sits on chaise longue with paper.

Thanks.

He drinks, sits back and sighs with contentment.

Aah.

SARAH. Tired?

RICHARD. Just a little.

SARAH. Bad traffic?

RICHARD. No. Quite good traffic, actually.

SARAH. Oh, good.

RICHARD. Very smooth.

Pause.

SARAH. It seemed to me you were just a little late.

RICHARD. Am I?

SARAH. Just a little.

RICHARD. There was a bit of a jam on the bridge.

SARAH *gets up, goes to drinks table to collect her glass, sits*
again on the chaise longue.

Pleasant day?

SARAH. Mmn. I was in the village this morning.

RICHARD. Oh yes? See anyone?

SARAH. Not really, no. Had lunch.

RICHARD. In the village?

SARAH. Yes.

RICHARD. Any good?

SARAH. Quite fair. (*She sits.*)

RICHARD. What about this afternoon? Pleasant afternoon?

SARAH. Oh yes. Quite marvellous.

RICHARD. Your lover came, did he?

SARAH. Mmnn. Oh yes.

RICHARD. Did you show him the hollyhocks?

Slight pause.

SARAH. The hollyhocks?

RICHARD. Yes.

SARAH. No, I didn't.

RICHARD. Oh.

SARAH. Should I have done?

RICHARD. No, no. It's simply that I seem to remember your saying he was interested in gardening.

SARAH. Mmnn, yes, he is.

Pause.

Not all that interested, actually.

RICHARD. Ah.

Pause.

Did you go out at all, or did you stay in?

SARAH. We stayed in.

RICHARD. Ah. (*He looks up at the Venetian blinds.*) That blind hasn't been put up properly.

SARAH. Yes, it is a bit crooked, isn't it?

Pause.

RICHARD. Very sunny on the road. Of course, by the time I got on to it the sun was beginning to sink. But I imagine it was quite warm here this afternoon. It was warm in the City.

SARAH. Was it?

RICHARD. Pretty stifling. I imagine it was quite warm everywhere.

SARAH. Quite a high temperature, I believe.

RICHARD. Did it say so on the wireless?

SARAH. I think it did, yes.

Slight pause.

RICHARD. One more before dinner?

SARAH. Mmn.

He pours drinks.

RICHARD. I see you had the Venetian blinds down.

SARAH. We did, yes.

RICHARD. The light was terribly strong.

SARAH. It was. Awfully strong.

RICHARD. The trouble with this room is that it catches the sun so directly, when it's shining. You didn't move to another room?

SARAH. No. We stayed here.

RICHARD. Must have been blinding.

SARAH. It was. That's why we put the blinds down.

Pause.

RICHARD. The thing is it gets so awfully hot in here with the blinds down.

SARAH. Would you say so?

RICHARD. Perhaps not. Perhaps it's just that you feel hotter.

SARAH. Yes. That's probably it.

Pause.

What did you do this afternoon?

RICHARD. Long meeting. Rather inconclusive.

SARAH. It's a cold supper. Do you mind?

RICHARD. Not in the least.

SARAH. I didn't seem to have time to cook anything today.

She moves towards the kitchen.

RICHARD. Oh, by the way . . . I rather wanted to ask you something.

SARAH. What?

RICHARD. Does it ever occur to you that while you're spending the afternoon being unfaithful to me I'm sitting at a desk going through balance sheets and graphs?

SARAH. What a funny question.

RICHARD. No, I'm curious.

SARAH. You've never asked me that before.

RICHARD. I've always wanted to know.

Slight pause.

SARAH. Well, of course it occurs to me.

RICHARD. Oh, it does?

SARAH. Mmnn.

Slight pause.

RICHARD. What's your attitude to that, then?

SARAH. It makes it all the more piquant.

RICHARD. Does it really?

SARAH. Of course.

RICHARD. You mean while you're with him . . . you actually have a picture of me, sitting at my desk going through balance sheets?

SARAH. Only at . . . certain times.

RICHARD. Of course.

SARAH. Not all the time.

RICHARD. Well, naturally.

SARAH. At particular moments.

RICHARD. Mmnn. But, in fact, I'm not completely forgotten?

SARAH. Not by any means.

RICHARD. That's rather touching, I must admit.

Pause.

SARAH. How could I forget you?

RICHARD. Quite easily, I should think.

SARAH. But I'm in your house.

RICHARD. With another.

SARAH. But it's you I love.

RICHARD. I beg your pardon?

SARAH. But it's you I love.

Pause. He looks at her, proffers his glass.

RICHARD. Let's have another drink.

She moves forward. He withdraws his glass, looks at her shoes.

What shoes are they?

SARAH. Mmnn?

RICHARD. Those shoes. They're unfamiliar. Very high-heeled, aren't they?

SARAH (*muttering*). Mistake. Sorry.

RICHARD (*not hearing*). Sorry? I beg your pardon?

SARAH. I'll . . . take them off.

RICHARD. Not quite the most comfortable shoes for an evening at home, I would have thought.

She goes into hall, opens cupboard, puts high-heeled shoes into cupboard, puts on low-heeled shoes. He moves to drinks table, pours himself a drink. She moves to centre table, lights a cigarette.

So you had a picture of me this afternoon, did you, sitting in my office?

SARAH. I did, yes. It wasn't a terribly convincing one, though.

RICHARD. Oh, why not?

SARAH. Because I knew you weren't there. I knew you were
with your mistress.

Pause.

RICHARD. Was I?

Short pause.

SARAH. Aren't you hungry?

RICHARD. I had a heavy lunch.

SARAH. How heavy?

He stands at the window.

RICHARD. What a beautiful sunset.

SARAH. Weren't you?

He turns and laughs.

RICHARD. What mistress?

SARAH. Oh, Richard . . .

RICHARD. No, no, it's simply the word that's so odd.

SARAH. Is it? Why?

Slight pause.

I'm honest with you, aren't I? Why can't you be honest
with me?

RICHARD. But I haven't got a mistress. I'm very well ac-
quainted with a whore, but I haven't got a mistress. There's
a world of difference.

SARAH. A whore?

RICHARD (*taking an olive*). Yes. Just a common or garden slut.
Not worth talking about. Handy between trains, nothing
more.

SARAH. You don't travel by train. You travel by car.

RICHARD. Quite. A quick cup of cocoa while they're checking
the oil and water.

Pause.

SARAH. Sounds utterly sterile.
RICHARD. No.

Pause.

SARAH. I must say I never expected you to admit it so readily.
RICHARD. Oh, why not? You've never put it to me so bluntly
   before, have you? Frankness at all costs. Essential to a
   healthy marriage. Don't you agree?
SARAH. Of course.
RICHARD. You agree.
SARAH. Entirely.
RICHARD. I mean, you're utterly frank with me, aren't you?
SARAH. Utterly.
RICHARD. About your lover. I must follow your example.
SARAH. Thank you.

Pause.

Yes, I have suspected it for some time.
RICHARD. Have you really?
SARAH. Mmnn.
RICHARD. Perceptive.
SARAH. But, quite honestly, I can't really believe she's just . . .
   what you say.
RICHARD. Why not?
SARAH. It's just not possible. You have such taste. You care
   so much for grace and elegance in women.
RICHARD. And wit.
SARAH. And wit, yes.
RICHARD. Wit, yes. Terribly important, wit, for a man.
SARAH. Is she witty?
RICHARD (*laughing*). These terms just don't apply. You can't
   sensibly inquire whether a whore is witty. It's of no signi-
   ficance whether she is or she isn't. She's simply a whore, a
   functionary who either pleases or displeases.

SARAH. And she pleases you?

RICHARD. Today she is pleasing. Tomorrow . . . ? One can't say.

He moves towards the bedroom door taking off his jacket.

SARAH. I must say I find your attitude to women rather alarming.

RICHARD. Why? I wasn't looking for your double, was I? I wasn't looking for a woman I could respect, as you, whom I could admire and love, as I do you. Was I? All I wanted was . . . how shall I put it . . . someone who could express and engender lust with all lust's cunning. Nothing more.

He goes into the bedroom, hangs his jacket up in the wardrobe, and changes into his slippers.
In the living-room SARAH *puts her drink down, hesitates and then follows into the bedroom.*

SARAH. I'm sorry your affair possesses so little dignity.

RICHARD. The dignity is in my marriage.

SARAH. Or sensibility.

RICHARD. The sensibility likewise. I wasn't looking for such attributes. I find them in you.

SARAH. Why did you look at all?

Slight pause.

RICHARD. What did you say?

SARAH. Why look . . . elsewhere . . . at all?

RICHARD. But my dear, you looked. Why shouldn't I look?

Pause.

SARAH. Who looked first?

RICHARD. You.

SARAH. I don't think that's true.

RICHARD. Who, then?

She looks at him with a slight smile.
Fade up. Night. Moonlight on balcony. The lights fade.
RICHARD *comes in bedroom door in his pyjamas. He picks up*
a book and looks at it. SARAH *comes from bathroom in her*
nightdress. There is a double bed. SARAH *sits at the dressing-*
table. Combs her hair.

SARAH. Richard?

RICHARD. Mnn?

SARAH. Do you ever think about me at all . . . when you're
with her?

RICHARD. Oh, a little. Not much.

　　Pause.

　We talk about you.

SARAH. You talk about me with her?

RICHARD. Occasionally. It amuses her.

SARAH. Amuses her?

RICHARD (*choosing a book*). Mmnn.

SARAH. How . . . do you talk about me?

RICHARD. Delicately. We discuss you as we would play an
antique music box. We play it for our titillation, whenever
desired.

　　Pause.

SARAH. I can't pretend the picture gives me great pleasure.

RICHARD. It wasn't intended to. The pleasure is mine.

SARAH. Yes, I see that, of course.

RICHARD (*sitting on the bed*). Surely your own afternoon
pleasures are sufficient for you, aren't they? You don't
expect extra pleasure from my pastimes, do you?

SARAH. No, not at all.

RICHARD. Then why all the questions?

SARAH. Well, it was you who started it. Asking me so many

questions about . . . my side of it. You don't normally do that.

RICHARD. Objective curiosity, that's all.

He touches her shoulders.

You're not suggesting I'm jealous, surely?

She smiles, stroking his hand.

SARAH. Darling. I know you'd never stoop to that.
RICHARD. Good God, no.

He squeezes her shoulder.

What about you? You're not jealous, are you?
SARAH. No. From what you tell me about your lady I seem to have a far richer time than you do.
RICHARD. Possibly.

He opens the windows fully and stands by them, looking out.

What peace. Come and look.

She joins him at the window.
They stand silently.

What would happen if I came home early one day, I wonder?

Pause.

SARAH. What would happen if I followed you one day, I wonder?

Pause.

RICHARD. Perhaps we could all meet for tea in the village.
SARAH. Why the village? Why not here?
RICHARD. Here? What an extraordinary remark.

Pause.

Your poor lover has never seen the night from this window, has he?

SARAH. No. He's obliged to leave before sunset, unfortunately.

RICHARD. Doesn't he get a bit bored with these damn afternoons? This eternal teatime? I would. To have as the constant image of your lust a milk jug and teapot. Must be terribly dampening.

SARAH. He's very adaptable. And, of course, when one puts the blinds down it does become a kind of evening.

RICHARD. Yes, I suppose it would.

Pause.

What does he think of your husband?

Slight pause.

SARAH. He respects you.

Pause.

RICHARD. I'm rather moved by that remark, in a strange kind of way. I think I can understand why you like him so much.

SARAH. He's terribly sweet.

RICHARD. Mmn-hmmnn.

SARAH. Has his moods, of course.

RICHARD. Who doesn't?

SARAH. But I must say he's very loving. His whole body emanates love.

RICHARD. How nauseating.

SARAH. No.

RICHARD. Manly with it, I hope?

SARAH. Entirely.

RICHARD. Sounds tedious.

SARAH. Not at all.

Pause.

He has a wonderful sense of humour.

RICHARD. Oh, jolly good. Makes you laugh, does he? Well,

mind the neighbours don't hear you. The last thing we want is gossip.

Pause.

SARAH. It's wonderful to live out here, so far away from the main road, so secluded.

RICHARD. Yes, I do agree.

They go back into the room. They get into the bed. He picks up his book and looks at it. He closes it and puts it down.

This isn't much good.

He switches off his bedside lamp. She does the same. Moonlight.

He's married, isn't he?

SARAH. Mmmmn.

RICHARD. Happily?

SARAH. Mmmmn.

Pause.

And you're happy, aren't you? You're not in any way jealous?

RICHARD. No.

SARAH. Good. Because I think things are beautifully balanced, Richard.

Fade.

Fade up. Morning. SARAH *putting on her negligee in the bedroom. She begins to make the bed.*

SARAH. Darling.

Pause.

Will the shears be ready this morning?

RICHARD (*in bathroom, off*). The what?

SARAH. The shears.

RICHARD. No, not this morning.

He enters, fully dressed in his suit. Kisses her on the cheek.

Not till Friday. Bye-bye.

He leaves the bedroom, collects hat and briefcase from hall.

SARAH. Richard.

He turns.

You won't be home too early today, will you?

RICHARD. Do you mean he's coming again today? Good gracious. He was here yesterday. Coming again today?

SARAH. Yes.

RICHARD. Oh. No, well, I won't be home early. I'll go to the National Gallery.

SARAH. Right.

RICHARD. Bye-bye.

SARAH. Bye.

The lights fade.
Fade up. Afternoon. SARAH *comes downstairs into living-room. She wears a very tight, low-cut black dress. She hastily looks at herself in the mirror. Suddenly notices she is wearing low-heeled shoes. She goes quickly to cupboard changes them for her high-heeled shoes. Looks again in mirror, smooths her hips. Goes to window, pulls venetian blinds down, opens them, and closes them until there is a slight slit of light. There are three chimes of a clock. She looks at her watch, goes towards the flowers on the table. Door bell. She goes to door. It is the milkman,* JOHN.

JOHN. Cream?

SARAH. You're very late.

JOHN. Cream?

SARAH. No, thank you.

JOHN. Why not?
SARAH. I have some. Do I owe you anything?
JOHN. Mrs. Owen just had three jars. Clotted.
SARAH. What do I owe you?
JOHN. It's not Saturday yet.
SARAH (*taking the milk*). Thank you.
JOHN. Don't you fancy any cream? Mrs. Owen had three jars.
SARAH. Thank you.

> *She closes the door. Goes into the kitchen with milk. Comes back with a tea-tray, holding teapot and cups, sets it on small table above chaise longue. She briefly attends to the flowers, sits on the chaise longue, crosses her legs, uncrosses them, puts her legs up on chaise longue, smooths her stockings under her skirt. The doorbell rings. Pulling her dress down she moves to the door, opens it.*

Hallo, Max.

> *RICHARD comes in. He is wearing a suede jacket, and no tie. He walks into the room and stands.*
> *She closes the door behind him. Walks slowly down past him, and sits on the chaise longue, crossing her legs.*
> *Pause.*
> *He moves slowly to chaise longue and stands very close to her at her back. She arches her back, uncrosses her legs, moves away to low chair down left.*
> *Pause.*
> *He looks at her, then moves towards the hall cupboard, brings out a bongo drum. He places the drum on the chaise longue, stands.*
> *Pause.*
> *She rises, moves past him towards the hall, turns, looks at him. He moves below chaise. They sit at either end. He begins to tap the drum. Her forefinger moves along drum towards his hand. She scratches the back of his hand sharply. Her hand retreats. Her fingers tap one after the other towards him, and*

rest. Her forefinger scratches between his fingers. Her other fingers do the same. His legs tauten. His hand clasps hers. Her hand tries to escape. Wild beats of their fingers tangling. Stillness.

She gets up, goes to drinks table, lights a cigarette, moves to window. He puts drum down on chair down right, picks up cigarette, moves to her.

MAX. Excuse me.

She glances at him and away.

Excuse me, have you got a light?

She does not respond.

Do you happen to have a light?

SARAH. Do you mind leaving me alone?

MAX. Why?

Pause.

I'm merely asking if you can give me a light.

She moves from him and looks up and down the room. He follows to her shoulder. She turns back.

SARAH. Excuse me.

*She moves past him. Close, his body follows.
She stops.*

I don't like being followed.

MAX. Just give me a light and I won't bother you. That's all I want.

SARAH (*through her teeth*). Please go away. I'm waiting for someone.

MAX. Who?

SARAH. My husband.

MAX. Why are you so shy? Eh? Where's your lighter?

He touches her body. An indrawn breath from her.

Here?

Pause.

Where is it?

He touches her body. A gasp from her.

Here?

She wrenches herself away. He traps her in the corner.

SARAH (*hissing*). What do you think you're doing?
MAX. I'm dying for a puff.
SARAH. I'm waiting for my husband!
MAX. Let me get a light from yours.

> *They struggle silently.*
> *She breaks away to wall.*
> *Silence.*
> *He approaches.*

Are you all right, miss? I've just got rid of that . . . gentle-
man. Did he hurt you in any way?
SARAH. Oh, how wonderful of you. No, no, I'm all right.
Thank you.
MAX. Very lucky I happened to be passing. You wouldn't
believe that could happen in such a beautiful park.
SARAH. No, you wouldn't.
MAX. Still, you've come to no harm.
SARAH. I can never thank you enough. I'm terribly grateful, I
really am.
MAX. Why don't you sit down a second and calm yourself.
SARAH. Oh, I'm quite calm – but . . . yes, thank you. You're
so kind. Where shall we sit.
MAX. Well, we can't sit out. It's raining. What about that
park-keeper's hut?

SARAH. Do you think we should? I mean, what about the park-keeper?

MAX. I am the park-keeper.

They sit on the chaise longue.

SARAH. I never imagined I could meet anyone so kind.

MAX. To treat a lovely young woman like you like that, it's unpardonable.

SARAH (*gazing at him*). You seem so mature, so . . . appreciative.

MAX. Of course.

SARAH. So gentle. So . . . Perhaps it was all for the best.

MAX. What do you mean?

SARAH. So that we could meet. So that we could meet. You and I.

Her fingers trace his thigh. He stares at them, lifts them off.

MAX. I don't quite follow you.

SARAH. Don't you?

Her fingers trace his thigh. He stares at them, lifts them off.

MAX. Now look, I'm sorry. I'm married.

She takes his hand and puts it on her knee.

SARAH. You're so sweet, you mustn't worry.

MAX (*snatching his hand away*). No, I really am. My wife's waiting for me.

SARAH. Can't you speak to strange girls?

MAX. No.

SARAH. Oh, how sickening you are. How tepid.

MAX. I'm sorry.

SARAH. You men are all alike. Give me a cigarette.

MAX. I bloody well won't.

SARAH. I beg your pardon?

MAX. Come here, Dolores.

SARAH. Oh no, not me. Once bitten twice shy, thanks. (*She stands.*) Bye-bye.

MAX. You can't get out, darling. The hut's locked. We're alone. You're trapped.

SARAH. Trapped! I'm a married woman. You can't treat me like this.

MAX (*moving to her*). It's teatime, Mary.

She moves swiftly behind the table and stands there with her back to the wall. He moves to the opposite end of the table, hitches his trousers, bends and begins to crawl under the table towards her.

He disappears under the velvet cloth. Silence. She stares down at the table. Her legs are hidden from view. His hand is on her leg. She looks about, grimaces, grits her teeth, gasps, gradually sinks under the table, and disappears. Long silence.

HER VOICE. Max!

Lights fade.
Fade up.
MAX sitting on chair down left.
SARAH pouring tea.

SARAH. Max.
MAX. What?
SARAH (*fondly*). Darling.

Slight pause.

What is it? You're very thoughtful.
MAX. No.
SARAH. You are. I know it.

Pause.

MAX. Where's your husband?

Pause.

SARAH. My husband? You know where he is.
MAX. Where?
SARAH. He's at work.
MAX. Poor fellow. Working away, all day.

Pause.

I wonder what he's like.
SARAH (*chuckling*). Oh, Max.
MAX. I wonder if we'd get on. I wonder if we'd . . . you know . . . hit it off.
SARAH. I shouldn't think so.
MAX. Why not?
SARAH. You've got very little in common.
MAX. Have we? He's certainly very accommodating. I mean, he knows perfectly well about these afternoons of ours, doesn't he?
SARAH. Of course.
MAX. He's known for years.

Slight pause.

Why does he put up with it?
SARAH. Why are you suddenly talking about him? I mean what's the point of it? It isn't a subject you normally elaborate on.
MAX. Why does he put up with it?
SARAH. Oh, shut up.
MAX. I asked you a question.

Pause.

SARAH. He doesn't mind.
MAX. Doesn't he?

Slight pause.

Well, I'm beginning to mind.

Pause.

SARAH. What did you say.
MAX. I'm beginning to mind.

Slight pause.

It's got to stop. It can't go on.
SARAH. Are you serious?

Silence.

MAX. It can't go on.
SARAH. You're joking.
MAX. No, I'm not.
SARAH. Why? Because of my husband? Not because of my husband, I hope. That's going a little far, I think.
MAX. No, nothing to do with your husband. It's because of my wife.

Pause.

SARAH. Your wife?
MAX. I can't deceive her any longer.
SARAH. Max . . .
MAX. I've been deceiving her for years. I can't go on with it. It's killing me.
SARAH. But darling, look –
MAX. Don't touch me.

Pause.

SARAH. What did you say?
MAX. You heard.

Pause.

SARAH. But your wife . . . knows. Doesn't she? You've told her . . . all about us. She's known all the time.
MAX. No, she doesn't know. She thinks I know a whore, that's all. Some spare-time whore, that's all. That's what she thinks.

SARAH. Yes, but be sensible . . . my love . . . she doesn't mind, does she?

MAX. She'd mind if she knew the truth, wouldn't she?

SARAH. What truth? What are you talking about?

MAX. She'd mind if she knew that, in fact . . . I've got a full-time mistress, two or three times a week, a woman of grace, elegance, wit, imagination –

SARAH. Yes, yes, you have –

MAX. In an affair that's been going on for years.

SARAH. She doesn't mind, she wouldn't mind – she's happy, she's happy.

Pause.

I wish you'd stop this rubbish, anyway.

She picks up the tea-tray and moves towards the kitchen.

You're doing your best to ruin the whole afternoon.

She takes the tray out. She then returns, looks at MAX *and goes to him.*

Darling. You don't really think you could have what we have with your wife, do you? I mean, my husband, for instance, completely appreciates that I –

MAX. How does he bear it, your husband? How does he bear it? Doesn't he smell me when he comes back in the evenings? What does he *say*? He must be mad. Now – what's the time – half-past four – now when he's sitting in his office, knowing what's going on here, what does he *feel*, how does he bear it?

SARAH. Max –

MAX. How?

SARAH. He's happy for me. He appreciates the way I am. He understands.

MAX. Perhaps I should meet him and have a word with him.

SARAH. Are you drunk?

MAX. Perhaps I should do that. After all, he's a man, like me. We're both men. You're just a bloody woman.

She slams the table.

SARAH. Stop it! What's the matter with you? What's happened to you? (*Quietly.*) Please, please, stop it. What are you doing, playing a game?

MAX. A game? I don't play games.

SARAH. Don't you? You do. Oh, you do. You do. Usually I like them.

MAX. I've played my last game.

SARAH. Why?

Slight pause.

MAX. The children.

Pause.

SARAH. What?

MAX. The children. I've got to think of the children.

SARAH. What children?

MAX. My children. My wife's children. Any minute now they'll be out of boarding school. I've got to think of them.

She sits close to him.

SARAH. I want to whisper something to you. Listen. Let me whisper to you. Mmmm? Can I? Please? It's whispering time. Earlier it was teatime, wasn't it? Wasn't it? Now it's whispering time.

Pause.

You like me to whisper to you. You like me to love you, whispering. Listen. You mustn't worry about . . . wives, husbands, things like that. It's silly. It's really silly. It's you, you now, here, here with me, here together, that's what it is, isn't it? You whisper to me, you take tea with me, you do that, don't you, that's what we are, that's us, love me.

He stands up.

MAX. You're too bony.

He walks away.

That's what it is, you see. I could put up with everything if it wasn't for that. You're too bony.

SARAH. Me? Bony? Don't be ridiculous.

MAX. I'm not.

SARAH. How can you say I'm bony?

MAX. Every move I make, your bones stick into me. I'm sick and tired of your bones.

SARAH. What are you talking about?

MAX. I'm telling you you're too bony.

SARAH. But I'm fat! Look at me. I'm plump anyway. You always told me I was plump.

MAX. You were plump once. You're not plump any more.

SARAH. Look at me.

He looks.

MAX. You're not plump enough. You're nowhere near plump enough. You know what I like. I like enormous women. Like bullocks with udders. Vast great uddered bullocks.

SARAH. You mean cows.

MAX. I don't mean cows. I mean voluminous great uddered feminine bullocks. Once, years ago, you vaguely resembled one.

SARAH. Oh, thanks.

MAX. But now, quite honestly, compared to my ideal . . .

He stares at her.

. . . you're skin and bone.

They stare at each other.
He puts on his jacket.

SARAH. You're having a lovely joke.
MAX. It's no joke.

He goes out. She looks after him. She turns, goes slowly towards the bongo drum, picks it up, puts it in the cupboard. She turns, looks at chaise a moment, walks slowly into the bedroom, sits on the end of the bed. The lights fade.
Fade up. Early evening. Six chimes of the clock. RICHARD comes in the front door. He is wearing his sober suit. He puts his briefcase in cupboard, hat on hook, looks about the room, pours a drink. SARAH comes into the bedroom from bathroom, wearing a sober dress. They both stand quite still in the two rooms for a few moments. SARAH moves to the balcony, looks out, RICHARD comes into the bedroom.

RICHARD. Hello.

Pause.

SARAH. Hello.
RICHARD. Watching the sunset?

He picks up a bottle.

Drink?
SARAH. Not at the moment, thank you.
RICHARD. Oh, what a dreary conference. Went on all day. Terribly fatiguing. Still, good work done, I think. Something achieved. Sorry I'm rather late. Had to have a drink with one or two of the overseas people. Good chaps.

He sits.

How are you?
SARAH. Fine.

RICHARD. Good.

Silence.

You seem a little depressed. Anything the matter?
SARAH. No.
RICHARD. What sort of day have you had?
SARAH. Not bad.
RICHARD. Not good?

Pause.

SARAH. Fair.
RICHARD. Oh, I'm sorry.

Pause.

Good to be home, I must say. You can't imagine what a comfort it·is.

Pause.

Lover come?

She does not reply.

Sarah?
SARAH. What? Sorry. I was thinking of something.
RICHARD. Did your lover come?
SARAH. Oh yes. He came.
RICHARD. In good shape?
SARAH. I have a headache actually.
RICHARD. Wasn't he in good shape?

Pause.

SARAH. We all have our off days.
RICHARD. He, too? I thought the whole point of being a lover is that one didn't. I mean if I, for instance, were called upon to fulfil the function of a lover and felt disposed, shall we say, to accept the job, well, I'd as soon give it up as be found incapable of executing its proper and consistent obligation.

SARAH. You do use long words.
RICHARD. Would you prefer me to use short ones?
SARAH. No, thank you.

Pause.

RICHARD. But I am sorry you had a bad day.
SARAH. It's quite all right.
RICHARD. Perhaps things will improve.
SARAH. Perhaps.

Pause.

I hope so.

She leaves the bedroom, goes into the living-room, lights a cigarette and sits. He follows.

RICHARD. Nevertheless, I find you very beautiful.
SARAH. Thank you.
RICHARD. Yes, I find you very beautiful. I have great pride in being seen with you. When we're out to dinner, or at the theatre.
SARAH. I'm so glad.
RICHARD. Or at the Hunt Ball.
SARAH. Yes, the Hunt Ball.
RICHARD. Great pride, to walk with you as my wife on my arm. To see you smile, laugh, walk, talk, bend, be still. To hear your command of contemporary phraseology, your delicate use of the very latest idiomatic expression, so subtly employed. Yes. To feel the envy of others, their attempts to gain favour with you, by fair means or foul, your austere grace confounding them. And to know you are my wife. It's a source of a profound satisfaction to me.

Pause.

What's for dinner.
SARAH. I haven't thought.

RICHARD. Oh, why not?

SARAH. I find the thought of dinner fatiguing. I prefer not to think about it.

RICHARD. That's rather unfortunate. I'm hungry.

Slight pause.

You hardly expect me to embark on dinner after a day spent sifting matters of high finance in the City.

She laughs.

One could even suggest you were falling down on your wifely duties.

SARAH. Oh dear.

RICHARD. I must say I rather suspected this would happen, sooner or later.

Pause.

SARAH. How's your whore?

RICHARD. Splendid.

SARAH. Fatter or thinner?

RICHARD. I beg your pardon?

SARAH. Is she fatter or thinner?

RICHARD. She gets thinner every day.

SARAH. That must displease you.

RICHARD. Not at all. I'm fond of thin ladies.

SARAH. I thought the contrary.

RICHARD. Really? Why would you have thought that?

Pause.

Of course, your failure to have dinner on the table is quite consistent with the life you've been leading for some time, isn't it?

SARAH. Is it?

RICHARD. Entirely.

Slight pause.

Perhaps I'm being unkind. Am I being unkind?
SARAH (*looks at him*). I don't know.
RICHARD. Yes, I am. In the traffic jam on the bridge just now, you see, I came to a decision.

Pause.

SARAH. Oh? What?
RICHARD. That it has to stop.
SARAH. What?
RICHARD. Your debauchery.

Pause.

Your life of depravity. Your path of illegitimate lust.
SARAH. Really?
RICHARD. Yes, I've come to an irrevocable decision on that point.

She stands.

SARAH. Would you like some cold ham?
RICHARD. Do you understand me?
SARAH. Not at all. I have something cold in the fridge.
RICHARD. Too cold, I'm sure. The fact is this is my house. From today, I forbid you to entertain your lover on these premises. This applies to any time of the day. Is that understood.
SARAH. I've made a salad for you.
RICHARD. Are you drinking?
SARAH. Yes, I'll have one.
RICHARD. What are you drinking?
SARAH. You know what I drink. We've been married ten years.
RICHARD. So we have.

He pours.

It's strange, of course, that it's taken me so long to appreciate the humiliating ignominy of my position.

SARAH. I didn't take my lover ten years ago. Not quite. Not on the honeymoon.

RICHARD. That's irrelevant. The fact is I am a husband who has extended to his wife's lover open house on any afternoon of her desire. I've been too kind. Haven't I been too kind?

SARAH. But of course. You're terribly kind.

RICHARD. Perhaps you would give him my compliments, by letter if you like, and ask him to cease his visits from (*He consults calendar.*) – the twelfth inst.

Long silence.

SARAH. How can you talk like this?

Pause.

Why today . . . so suddenly?

Pause.

Mmmm?

She is close to him.

You've had a hard day . . . at the office. All those overseas people. It's so tiring. But it's silly, it's so silly, to talk like this. I'm here. For you. And you've always appreciated . . . how much these afternoons . . . mean. You've always understood.

She presses her cheek to his.

Understanding is so rare, so dear.

RICHARD. Do you think it's pleasant to know that your wife is unfaithful to you two or three times a week, with great regularity?

SARAH. Richard –

RICHARD. It's insupportable. It has become insupportable.
I'm no longer disposed to put up with it.

SARAH (*to him*). Sweet . . . Richard . . . please.

RICHARD. Please what?

She stops.

Can I tell you what I suggest you do?

SARAH. What?

RICHARD. Take him out into the fields. Find a ditch. Or a
slag heap. Find a rubbish dump. Mmmm? What about
that?

She stands still.

Buy a canoe and find a stagnant pond. Anything. Anywhere.
But not my living-room.

SARAH. I'm afraid that's not possible.

RICHARD. Why not?

SARAH. I said it's not possible.

RICHARD. But if you want your lover so much, surely that's the
obvious thing to do, since his entry to this house is now
barred. I'm trying to be helpful, darling, because of my love
for you. You can see that. If I find him on these premises I'll
kick his teeth out.

SARAH. You're mad.

He stares at her.

RICHARD. I'll kick his head in.

Pause.

SARAH. What about your own bloody whore?

RICHARD. I've paid her off.

SARAH. Have you? Why?

RICHARD. She was too bony.

Slight pause.

SARAH. But you liked . . . you said you liked . . . Richard . . . but you love me . . .

RICHARD. Of course.

SARAH. Yes . . . you love me . . . you don't mind him . . . you understand him . . . don't you ? . . . I mean, you know better than I do . . . darling . . . all's well . . . all's well . . . the evenings . . . and the afternoons . . . do you see ? Listen, I do have dinner for you. It's ready. I wasn't serious. It's Boeuf bourgignon. And tomorrow I'll have Chicken Chasseur. Would you like it ?

They look at each other.

RICHARD (*softly*). Adulteress.

SARAH. You can't talk like this, it's impossible, you know you can't. What do you think you're doing ?

He remains looking at her for a second, then moves into the hall.
He opens the hall cupboard and takes out the bongo drum. She watches him.
He returns.

RICHARD. What's this ? I found it some time ago. What is it ?

Pause.

What is it ?

SARAH. You shouldn't touch that.

RICHARD. But it's in my house. It belongs either to me, or to you, or to another.

SARAH. It's nothing. I bought it in a jumble sale. It's nothing. What do you think it is ? Put it back.

RICHARD. Nothing ? This ? A drum in my cupboard ?

SARAH. Put it back!

RICHARD. It isn't by any chance anything to do with your illicit afternoons ?

SARAH. Not at all. Why should it?
RICHARD. It is used. This is used, isn't it? I can guess.
SARAH. You guess nothing. Give it to me.
RICHARD. How does he use it? How do you use it? Do you
play it while I'm at the office?

*She tries to take the drum. He holds on to it. They are still,
hands on the drum.*

What function does this fulfil? It's not just an ornament, I
take it? What do you do with it?
SARAH (*with quiet anguish*). You've no right to question me.
No right at all. It was our arrangement. No questions of this
kind. Please. Don't, don't. It was our arrangement.
RICHARD. I want to know.

She closes her eyes.

SARAH. Don't . . .
RICHARD. Do you both play it? Mmmmnn? Do you both
play it? Together?

She moves away swiftly, then turns, hissing.

SARAH. You stupid . . .! (*She looks at him coolly.*) Do you think
he's the only one who comes! Do you? Do you think he's the
only one I entertain? Mmmnn? Don't be silly. I have other
visitors, other visitors, all the time, I receive all the time.
Other afternoons, all the time. When neither of you know,
neither of you. I give them strawberries in season. With
cream. Strangers, total strangers. But not to me, not while
they're here. They come to see the hollyhocks. And then they
stay for tea. Always. Always.
RICHARD. Is that so?

*He moves towards her, tapping the drum gently.
He faces her, tapping, then grasps her hand and scratches it
across the drum.*

SARAH. What are you doing?
RICHARD. Is that what you do?

>*She jerks away, to behind the table.*
>*He moves towards her, tapping.*

Like that?

>*Pause.*

What fun.

>*He scratches the drum sharply and then places it on the*
>*chair.*

Got a light?

>*Pause.*

Got a light?

>*She retreats towards the table, eventually ending behind it.*

Come on, don't be a spoilsport. Your husband won't mind,
if you give me a light. You look a little pale. Why are you
so pale? A lovely girl like you.
SARAH. Don't, don't say that!
RICHARD. You're trapped. We're alone. I've locked up.
SARAH. You mustn't do this, you mustn't do it, you mustn't!
RICHARD. He won't mind.

>*He begins to move slowly closer to the table.*

No one else knows.

>*Pause.*

No one else can hear us. No one knows we're here.

>*Pause.*

Come on. Give us a light.

Pause.

You can't get out, darling. You're trapped.

They face each other from opposite ends of the table.
She suddenly giggles.
Silence.

SARAH. I'm trapped.

Pause.

What will my husband say?

Pause.

He expects me. He's waiting. I can't get out. I'm trapped. You've no right to treat a married woman like this. Have you? Think, think, think of what you're doing.

She looks at him, bends and begins to crawl under the table towards him. She emerges from under the table and kneels at his feet, looking up. Her hand goes up his leg. He is looking down at her.

You're very forward. You really are. Oh, you really are. But my husband will understand. My husband does understand. Come here. Come down here. I'll explain. After all, think of my marriage. He adores me. Come here and I'll whisper to you. I'll whisper it. It's whispering time. Isn't it?

She takes his hands. He sinks to his knees, with her. They are kneeling together, close. She strokes his face.

It's a very late tea. Isn't it? But I think I like it. Aren't you sweet? I've never seen you before after sunset. My husband's at a late-night conference. Yes, you look different. Why are you wearing this strange suit, and this tie? You usually wear something else, don't you? Take off your jacket. Mmmnn? Would you like me to change? Would you like me to change my clothes? I'll change for you, darling. Shall I? Would you like that?

Silence. She is very close to him.

RICHARD. Yes.

Pause.

Change.

Pause.

Change.

Pause.

Change your clothes.

Pause.

You lovely whore.

They are still, kneeling, she leaning over him.

TEA PARTY

TEA PARTY was commissioned by sixteen member countries of the European Broadcasting Union, to be transmitted by all of them under the title, *The Largest Theatre in the World*. It was first presented by B.B.C. Television on 25 March 1965 with the following cast:

DISSON	Leo McKern
WENDY	Vivien Merchant
DIANA	Jennifer Wright
WILLY	Charles Gray
DISLEY	John Le Mesurier
LOIS	Margaret Denyer
FATHER	Frederick Piper
MOTHER	Hilda Barry
TOM	Peter Bartlett
JOHN	Robert Bartlett

Directed by Charles Jarrott

An electric lift.
An electric lift rising to the top floor of an office block. WENDY
stands in it.

Corridor. .
The lift comes to rest in a broad carpeted corridor, the interior of
an office suite. It is well appointed, silent. The walls are papered
with Japanese silk. Along the walls in alcoves are set, at various
intervals, a selection of individually designed wash basins, water
closets and bidets, all lit by hooded spotlights.
WENDY *steps out of the lift and walks down the corridor towards*
a door. She knocks. It opens.

Disson's office. Morning.
DISSON *rising from a large desk. He goes round the desk to meet*
WENDY *and shakes her hand.*
DISSON. How do you do, Miss Dodd? Nice of you to come.
    Please sit down.
        DISSON *goes back to his seat behind the desk.* WENDY *sits*
        in a chair at the corner of the desk.
    That's right.
        He refers to papers on the desk.
    Well now, I've had a look at your references. They seem to
    be excellent. You've had quite a bit of experience.
WENDY. Yes, sir.
DISSON. Not in my line, of course. We manufacture sanitary
    ware . . . but I suppose you know that?
WENDY. Yes, of course I do, Mr Disson.
DISSON. You've heard of us, have you?
WENDY. Oh yes.
        WENDY *crosses her left leg over her right.*

DISSON   Well, do you think you'd be interested in . . . in this area of work?

WENDY. Oh, certainly, sir, yes, I think I would.

DISSON. We're the most advanced sanitary engineers in the country. I think I can say that quite confidently.

WENDY. Yes, I believe so.

DISSON. Oh yes. We manufacture more bidets than anyone else in England. (*He laughs.*) It's almost by way of being a mission. Cantilever units, hidden cisterns, footpedals, you know, things like that.

WENDY. Footpedals?

DISSON. Instead of a chain or plug. A footpedal.

WENDY. Oh. How marvellous.

DISSON. They're growing more popular every day and rightly so.

> WENDY *crosses her right leg over her left.*

Well now, this . . . post is, in fact, that of my personal assistant. Did you understand that? A very private secretary, in fact. And a good deal of responsibility would undoubtedly devolve upon you. Would you . . . feel yourself capable of discharging it?

WENDY. Once I'd correlated all the fundamental features of the work, sir, I think so, yes.

DISSON. All the fundamental features, yes. Good.

> WENDY *crosses her left leg over her right.*

I see you left your last job quite suddenly.

> *Pause.*

May I ask the reason?

WENDY. Well, it's . . . a little embarrassing, sir.

DISSON. Really?

> *Pause.*

Well, I think I should know, don't you? Come on, you can tell me. What was it?

> WENDY *straightens her skirt over her knees.*

WENDY. Well, it is rather personal, Mr Disson.

DISSON. Yes, but I think I should know, don't you?
Pause.
WENDY. Well, it's simply that I couldn't persuade my chief . . .
to call a halt to his attentions.
DISSON. *What?* (*He consults the papers on the desk.*) A firm of
this repute? It's unbelievable.
WENDY. I'm afraid it's true, sir.
Pause.
DISSON. What sort of attentions?
WENDY. Oh, I don't . . .
DISSON. What sort?
Pause.
WENDY. He never stopped touching me, Mr Disson, that's all.
DISSON. Touching you?
WENDY. Yes.
DISSON. Where? (*Quickly.*) That must have been very dis-
turbing for you.
WENDY. Well, quite frankly, it is disturbing, to be touched all
the time.
DISSON. Do you mean at every opportunity?
WENDY. Yes, sir.
Slight pause.
DISSON. Did you cry?
WENDY. Cry?
DISSON. Did he make you cry?
WENDY. Oh, just a little, occasionally, sir.
DISSON. What a monster.
Slight pause.
Well, I do sympathize.
WENDY. Thank you, sir.
DISSON. One would have thought this . . . tampering, this . . .
interfering . . . with secretaries was something of the past, a
myth, in fact, something that only took place in paperback
books. Tch. Tch.
WENDY *crosses her right leg over her left.*

Anyway, be that as it may, your credentials are excellent and I would say you possessed an active and inquiring intelligence and a pleasing demeanour, two attributes I consider necessary for this post. I'd like you to start immediately.

WENDY. Oh, that's wonderful. Thank you so much, Mr Disson.

DISSON. Not at all.

They stand. He walks across the room to another desk.

This'll be your desk.

WENDY. Ah.

DISSON. There are certain personal arrangements I'd like you to check after lunch. I'm . . . getting married tomorrow.

WENDY. Oh, congratulations.

DISSON. Thanks. Yes, this is quite a good week for me, what with one thing and another.

The telephone rings on his desk.

He crosses and picks it up.

Hullo, Disley. How are you? . . . What? Oh my goodness, don't say that.

Disson's house. Sitting-room. Evening.

DIANA. This is my brother Willy.

DISSON. I'm very glad to meet you.

WILLY. And I you. Congratulations.

DISSON. Thank you.

DIANA (*giving him a drink*). Here you are, Robert.

DISSON. Thanks. Cheers.

DIANA. Cheers.

WILLY. To tomorrow.

DISSON. Yes.

They drink.

I'm afraid we've run into a bit of trouble.

DIANA. Why?

DISSON. I've lost my best man.

DIANA. Oh no.

DISSON (*to* WILLY). My oldest friend. Man called Disley. Gastric flu. Can't make it tomorrow.

WILLY. Oh dear.

DISSON. He was going to make a speech at the reception – in my honour. A superb speech. I read it. Now he can't make it.
Pause.

WILLY. Isn't there anyone else you know?

DISSON. Yes, of course. But not like him . . . you see. I mean, he was the natural choice.

DIANA. How infuriating.
Pause.

WILLY. Well, look, I can be your best man, if you like.

DIANA. How can you, Willy? You're giving me away.

WILLY. Oh yes.

DISSON. Oh, the best man's not important; you can always get a best man – all he's got to do is stand there; it's the speech that's important, the speech in honour of the groom. Who's going to make the speech?
Pause.

WILLY. Well, I can make the speech, if you like.

DISSON. But how can you make a speech in honour of the groom when you're making one in honour of the bride?

WILLY. Does that matter?

DIANA. No. Why does it?

DISSON. Yes, but look . . . I mean, thanks very much . . . but the fact is . . . that you don't know me, do you? I mean we've only just met. Disley knows me well, that's the thing, you see. His speech centred around our long-standing friendship. I mean, what he knew of my character . . .

WILLY. Yes, of course, of course. No, look, all I'm saying is that I'm willing to have a crack at it if there's no other solution. Willing to come to the aid of the party, as it were.

DIANA. He *is* a wonderful speaker, Robert.

Wedding reception. Private room. Exclusive restaurant.

DISSON, DIANA, WILLY, DISSON'S PARENTS, DISSON'S
SONS. WILLY *is speaking.*

WILLY. I remember the days my sister and I used to swim together in the lake at Sunderley. The grace of her crawl, even then, as a young girl. I can remember those long summer evenings at Sunderley, my mother and I crossing the lawn towards the terrace and through the great windows hearing my sister play Brahms. The delicacy of her touch. My mother and I would, upon entering the music room, gaze in silence at Diana's long fingers moving in exquisite motion on the keys. As for our father, our father knew no pleasure keener than watching his daughter at her needlework. A man whose business was the State's, a man eternally active, his one great solace from the busy world would be to sit for hours on end at a time watching his beloved daughter ply her needle. Diana – my sister – was the dear grace of our household, the flower, the blossom, and the bloom. One can only say to the groom: Groom, your fortune is immeasurable.

Applause. DIANA *kisses him.*

DISSON *shakes his hand warmly.*

TOASTMASTER. My lords, reverend gentlemen, ladies and gentlemen, pray silence for Mr William Pierrepoint Torrance, who will propose the toast in honour of the groom.

WILLY *turns. Applause.*

WILLY. I have not known Robert for a long time, in fact I have known him only for a very short time. But in that short time I have found him to be a man of integrity, honesty and humility. After a modest beginning, he has built his business up into one of the proudest and most vigorous in the land. And this—almost alone. Now he has married a girl who equals, if not surpasses, his own austere standards of integrity. He has married my sister, who possesses within her that rare and uncommon attribute known as inner beauty not to mention the loveliness of her exterior. Par excellence as a woman with a needle, beyond excellence as a woman of taste, discernment, sensibility and imagination. An excellent swimmer who, in all probability, has the beating of her husband in the two hundred metres breast stroke.

Laughter and applause.

WILLY *waits for silence.*

It is to our parents that she owes her candour, her elegance of mind, her *sensibilité*. Our parents, who, though gone, have not passed from us, but who are here now on this majestic day, and offer you their welcome, the bride their love, and the groom their congratulations.

Applause. DIANA *kisses him.*

DISSON *shakes his hand warmly.*

DISSON. Marvellous.

WILLY. Diana, I want to tell you something.

DIANA. What?

WILLY. You have married a good man. He will make you happy.

DIANA. I know.

DISSON. Wonderful speeches. Wonderful. Listen. What are you doing these days?

WILLY. Nothing much.

TOASTMASTER. My lords . . .

DISSON (*whispering*). How would you like to come in with me for a bit? See how you like it, how you get on. Be my second in command. Office of your own. Plenty of room for initiative.

TOASTMASTER. My lords, reverend gentlemen, ladies and gentlemen –

WILLY. Marvellous idea. I'll say yes at once.

DISSON. Good.

DIANA *kisses* DISSON.

DIANA. Darling.

TOASTMASTER. Pray silence for the groom.

DISSON *moves forward.*

Applause. Silence.

DISSON. This is the happiest day of my life.

Sumptuous hotel room. Italy.
The light is on. The camera rests at the foot of the bed. The characters are not seen. Their voices heard only.

DISSON. Are you happy?

DIANA. Yes.

DISSON. Very happy?

DIANA. Yes.

DISSON. Have you ever been happier? With any other man?

DIANA. Never.

    Pause.

DISSON. I make you happy, don't I? Happier than you've ever been . . . with any other man.

DIANA. Yes. You do.

    Pause.

Yes.

    Silence.

Disson's house. Workroom.
DISSON *at his workbench. With sandpaper and file he is putting the finishing touches to a home-made model yacht. He completes the job, dusts the yacht, sets it on a shelf and looks at it with satisfaction.*

Disson's house. Breakfast room. Morning.
DISSON *and* DIANA *at the table.*
DISSON. Your eyes are shining.

    Pause.

They're shining.

DIANA. Mmmnnn.

DISSON. They've been shining for months.

DIANA (*smiling*). My eyes? Have they?

DISSON. Every morning.

Pause.

I'm glad you didn't marry that . . . Jerry . . . whatever-hisnamewas . . .

DIANA. Oh, him . . .

DISSON. Why didn't you?

DIANA. He was weak.

Pause.

DISSON. I'm not weak.

DIANA. No.

DISSON. Am I?

He takes her hand.

DIANA. You're strong.

THE TWINS *enter the room.*

THE TWINS *mutter*, 'Morning'.

DIANA *and* DISSON *say*, 'Good Morning'.

Silence. THE TWINS *sit.* DIANA *pours tea for them. They butter toast, take marmalade, begin to eat.*

Silence.

Would you like eggs?

TOM. No, thanks.

DIANA. John?

Silence.

DISSON. John!

JOHN. What?

DISSON. Don't say what!

JOHN. What shall I say?

DIANA. Would you like eggs?

Pause.

JOHN. Oh.

Pause.

No, thanks.

The boys giggle and eat. Silence.
JOHN *whispers to* TOM.

DISSON. What are you saying? Speak up.

JOHN. Nothing.

DISSON. Do you think I'm deaf?

TOM. I've never thought about it.

DISSON. I wasn't talking to you. I was talking to John.

JOHN. Me? Sorry, sir.

DISSON. Now don't be silly. You've never called me sir before.
That's rather a daft way to address your father.

JOHN. Uncle Willy called his father sir. He told me.

DISSON. Yes, but you don't call *me* sir! Do you understand?

Willy's office. Morning.
DISSON *leads* WILLY *in.*

DISSON. Here you are, Willy. This'll be your office. How'd
you like it?

WILLY. First rate.

DISSON. These two offices are completely cut off from the rest
of the staff. They're all on the lower floor. Our only contact
is by intercom, unless I need to see someone personally,
which is rare. Equally, I dislike fraternization between the
two offices. We shall meet only by strict arrangement, otherwise we'll never get any work done. That suit you?

WILLY. Perfectly.

DISSON. There was a man in here, but I got rid of him.

DISSON *leads* WILLY *through a communicating door into
his own office.*

Disson's office.
On a side table coffee is set for two.
DISSON *goes to the table and pours.*

DISSON. I think I should explain to you the sort of man I am.

I'm a thorough man. I like things to be done and done well.
I don't like dithering. I don't like indulgence. I don't like
self-doubt. I don't like fuzziness. I like clarity. Clear inten-
tion. Precise execution. Black or white?

WILLY. White, please.

DISSON. But I've no patience with conceit and self-regard. A
man's job is to assess his powers coolly and correctly and
equally the powers of others. Having done this, he can pro-
ceed to establish a balanced and reasonable relationship with
his fellows. In my view, living is a matter of active and willing
participation. So is work. Sugar?

WILLY. Two, please.

DISSON. Now, dependence isn't a word I would use lightly,
but I will use it and I don't regard it as a weakness. To understand the meaning of the term dependence is to understand
that one's powers are limited and that to live with others is
not only sensible but the only way work can be done and
dignity achieved. Nothing is more sterile or lamentable than
the man content to live within himself. I've always made it
my business to be on the most direct possible terms with the
members of my staff and the body of my business associates.
And by my example opinions are declared freely, without
shame or deception. It seems to me essential that we cultivate
the ability to operate lucidly upon our problems and there-
fore be in a position to solve them. That's why your sister
loves me. I don't play about at the periphery of matters. I
go right to the centre. I believe life can be conducted
efficiently. I never waste my energies in any kind of timorous
expectation. Neither do I ask to be loved. I expect to be
given only what I've worked for. If you make a plum pudding,
what do you do with it? You don't shove it up on a shelf.
You stick a knife into it and eat it. Everything has a function.
In other words, if we're to work together we must appreciate
that interdependence is the key word, that it's your job to
understand me and mine to understand you. Agreed?

WILLY. Absolutely.

DISSON. Now, the first thing you need is a secretary. We'll get on to it at once.

WILLY. Can I suggest someone? I know she's very keen and, I'd say, very competent.

DISSON. Who?

WILLY. My sister.

Pause.

DISSON. Your sister? You mean my wife?

WILLY. She told me she'd love to do it.

DISSON. She hasn't told me.

WILLY. She's shy.

DISSON. But she doesn't need to work. Why should she want to work?

WILLY. To be closer to you.

Willy's office.

WILLY *and* DIANA *at their desks, both examining folders intently. Silence.*

Disson's office.

DISSON *and* WENDY *at their desks.* WENDY *typing on an electric typewriter.* DISSON *looking out of the window.* DISSON *turns from the window, glances at the door leading to* WILLY'S *office. The intercom buzzes on* WENDY'S *desk. She switches through.*

WENDY. Mr Disson does not want to be disturbed until 3.30.

   DISSON *glances again at* WILLY'S *door.*
   Silence.

Disson's house. Sitting-room. Early evening.

DIANA *and* THE TWINS *are sitting about, reading.*

DIANA. Do you miss your mother?

JOHN. We didn't know her very well. We were very young when she died.

DIANA. Your father has looked after you and brought you up very well.

JOHN. Oh, thank you. He'll be pleased to hear that.

DIANA. I've told him.

JOHN. What did he say?

DIANA. He was pleased I thought so. You mean a great deal to him.

JOHN. Children seem to mean a great deal to their parents, I've noticed. Though I've often wondered what 'a great deal' means.

TOM. I've often wondered what 'mean' means.

DIANA. Aren't you proud of your father's achievements?

JOHN. We are. I should say we are.

Pause.

DIANA. And now that your father has married again . . . has the change in your life affected you very much?

JOHN. What change?

DIANA. Living with me.

JOHN. Ah. Well, I think there definitely is an adjustment to be made. Wouldn't you say that, Tom?

DIANA. Of course there is. But would you say it's an easy adjustment to make, or difficult?

JOHN. Well, it really all depends on how good you are at making adjustments. We're very good at making adjustments, aren't we, Tom?

The front door slams. DIANA *and* THE TWINS *look down at their books.* DISSON *comes in. They all look up, smile.*

DISSON. Hullo.

They all smile genially at him.

DISSON *looks quickly from one to the other.*

Disson's office. Morning.

Sun shining in the window. DISSON *at his desk.* WENDY
at the cabinet. He watches her. She turns.

WENDY. Isn't it a beautiful day, Mr Disson?

DISSON. Close the curtains.

> WENDY *closes the curtains.*

Got your pad?

WENDY. Yes, sir.

DISSON. Sit down.

> WENDY *sits in a chair by the corner of his desk.*

Warwick and Sons. We duly acknowledge receipt of your
letter of the twenty-first inst. There should be no difficulty
in meeting your requirements. What's the matter?

WENDY. Sir?

DISSON. You're wriggling.

WENDY. I'm sorry, sir.

DISSON. Is it the chair?

WENDY. Mmn . . . it might be.

DISSON. Too hard, I expect. A little hard for you.

> *Pause.*

Is that it?

WENDY. A little.

DISSON. Sit on the desk.

WENDY. The desk?

DISSON. Yes, on the leather.

> *Slight pause.*

It'll be softer . . . for you.

WENDY. Well, that'll be nice.

> *Pause.* WENDY *eventually uncrosses her legs and stands. She
> looks at the desk.*

I think it's a little high . . . to get up on.

DISSON. Of course it isn't.

WENDY (*looking at the desk*). Hmmmn-mmmn . . .

DISSON. Go on, get up. You couldn't call that high.

WENDY *places her back to the desk and slowly attempts to raise herself up on to it.*
She stops.

WENDY. I think I'll have to put my feet on the chair, really, to hoist myself up.

DISSON. You can hoist yourself up without using your feet.

WENDY (*dubiously*). Well . . .

DISSON. Look, get up or stay down. Make up your mind. One thing or the other. I want to get on with my letter to Birmingham.

WENDY. I was just wondering if you'd mind if I put my high-heeled shoes on your chair . . . to help me get up.
Pause.

DISSON. I don't mind.

WENDY. But I'm worried in case my heels might chip the wood. They're rather sharp, these heels.

DISSON. Are they?
Pause.
Well, try it, anyway. You won't chip the wood.

WENDY *puts her feet on the chair and hoists herself up on to the desk.*
He watches.
WENDY *settles herself on the desk and picks up her pen and pad. She reads from the pad.*

WENDY. There should be no difficulty in meeting your requirements.

Disson's house. Games room. Day.
DISSON *and* WILLY *are playing ping-pong.* THE TWINS *watch.*
A long rally. DISSON *backhand flips to win the point.*

JOHN. Good shot, Dad.

TOM. Thirteen–eighteen.

WILLY. Your backhand's in form, Robert.

JOHN. Attack his forehand.

WILLY *serves. A rally.* WILLY *attacks* DISSON'S *forehand.*
DISSON *moves over to his right and then flips backhand to*
win the point. THE TWINS *applaud.*

TOM. Thirteen–nineteen.

WILLY. Backhand flip on the forehand, eh?

WILLY *serves.*

From DISSON'S *point of view see two balls bounce and leap*
past both ears.

TWINS. Shot!

TOM. Fourteen–nineteen.

DISSON *puts down his bat and walks slowly to* WILLY.

DISSON. You served two balls, old chap.

WILLY. Two balls?

DISSON. You sent me two balls.

WILLY. No, no. Only one.

DISSON. Two.

Pause.

JOHN. One, Dad.

DISSON. What?

TOM. One.

Pause.

WILLY *walks to* DISSON'S *end, bends.*

WILLY. Look.

WILLY *picks up one ball.*

One ball. Catch!

He throws the ball. DISSON *gropes, loses sight of the ball.*
It bounces under the table. He crouches, leans under the table
for it. Gets it, withdraws, looks up. WILLY *and* THE TWINS
look down at him.

Disley's surgery.
Room darkened.
A torch shining in DISSON'S *eyes. First the left eye, then the right*
eye. Torch out. Light on.

DISLEY. There's nothing wrong with your eyes, old boy.

DISSON. Nothing?

DISLEY. They're in first-rate condition. Truly.

DISSON. That's funny.

DISLEY. I'd go as far as to say your sight was perfect.

DISSON. Huh.

DISLEY. Check the bottom line.

>DISLEY *switches off the light, puts on the light on the letter board.*

What is it?

DISSON. EXJLNVCGTY.

DISLEY. Perfect.

>*Board light off. Room light on.*

DISSON. Yes, I know . . . I know that . . .

DISLEY. Well, what are you worried about?

DISSON. It's not that . . .

DISLEY. Colour? Do you confuse colours? Look at me. What colour am I?

DISSON. Colourless.

DISLEY (*laughs, stops*). Very funny. What distinguishing marks can you see about me?

DISSON. Two.

DISLEY. What?

DISSON. You have one grey strip in your hair, quite faint.

DISLEY. Good. What's the other?

DISSON. You have a brown stain in your left cheek.

DISLEY. A brown stain? Can you see that? (*He looks in the mirror.*) I didn't know it was so evident.

DISSON. Of course it's evident. It stains your face.

DISLEY. Don't . . . go on about it, old boy. I didn't realize it was so evident. No one's ever noticed it before.

DISSON. Not even your wife?

DISLEY. Yes, she has. Anyway, I'd say your eyes are sharp enough. What colour are those lampshades?

DISSON. They're dark blue drums. Each has a golden rim. The carpet is Indian.

DISLEY. That's not a colour.

DISSON. It's white. Over there, by that cabinet, I can see a deep black burn.

DISLEY. A burn? Where? Do you mean that shadow?

DISSON. That's not a shadow. It's a burn.

DISLEY (*looking*). So it is. How the hell did that happen?

DISSON. Listen . . . I never said I couldn't see. You don't understand. Most of the time . . . my eyesight is excellent. It always has been. But . . . it's become unreliable. It's become . . . erratic. Sometimes, quite suddenly, very occasionally, something happens . . . something . . . goes wrong . . . with my eyes.

Pause.

DISLEY. I can find no evidence that your sight is in any way deficient.

DISSON. You don't understand.

A knock at the door. LOIS *appears.*

LOIS. I'm just going out. Wanted to say hullo to you before I go.

DISSON. Hullo, Lois.

He kisses her cheek.

LOIS. You've been in here for ages. Don't tell me you need glasses?

DISLEY. His eyes are perfect.

LOIS. They look it.

DISSON. What a lovely dress you're wearing.

LOIS. Do you like it? Really?

DISSON. Of course I like it.

LOIS. You must see if the birds are still there.

She lifts the blind.

Yes, they are. They're all at the bird bath.

They all look into the garden.

Look at them. They're so happy. They love my bath. They do, really. They love it. They make me so happy, my birds. And they seem to know, instinctively, that I adore them. They do, really.

Disson's house. Bedroom. Night.
DISSON *alone, in front of a mirror.*
He is tying his tie. He ties it. The front end hangs only half-way down his chest.
He unties it, ties it again. The front end, this time, is even shorter. He unties it, holds the tie and looks at it.
He then ties the tie again. This time the two ends are of equal length.
He breathes deeply, relaxes, goes out of the room.

Disson's house. Dining room. Night.
DIANA, WILLY, DISSON *at dinner.*
DIANA. I'd say she was a real find.
WILLY. Oh, she's of inestimable value to the firm, wouldn't you say, Robert?
DISSON. Oh yes.
DIANA. I mean for someone who's not . . . actually . . . part of us . . . I mean, an outsider . . . to give such devotion and willingness to the job, as she does . . . well, it's remarkable. We were very lucky to find her.
DISSON. I found her, actually.
WILLY. You found me, too, old boy.
DIANA (*laughing*). And me.
    Pause.
    She's, of course, so completely trustworthy, and so very persuasive, on the telephone. I've heard her . . . when the door's been open . . . once or twice.
WILLY. Oh, splendid girl, all round.
DISSON. She's not so bloody marvellous.
    Pause. They look at him.
    She's all right, she's all right. But she's not so bloody marvellous.

DIANA. Well, perhaps not quite as accomplished as I am, no. Do you think I'm a good private secretary, Willy?

WILLY. First rate.

Pause. They eat and drink.

DISSON. I don't think it's a good idea for you to work.

DIANA. Me? Why not? I love it.

DISSON. I never see you. If you were at home I could take the occasional afternoon off . . . to see you. As it is I never see you. In day-time.

DIANA. You mean I'm so near and yet so far?

Pause.

DISSON. Yes.

DIANA. Would you prefer me to be your secretary?

DISSON. No, no, of course not. That wouldn't work at all.

Pause.

WILLY. But we do all meet at lunch-time. We meet in the evening.

DISSON *looks at him.*

DIANA. But I like working. You wouldn't want me to work for someone else, would you, somewhere else?

DISSON. I certainly wouldn't. You know what Wendy told me, don't you?

DIANA. What?

DISSON. She told me her last employer was always touching her.

WILLY. No?

DISSON. Always. Touching her.

DIANA. Her body, you mean?

DISSON. What else?

Pause.

DIANA. Well, if we're to take it that that's general practice, I think it's safer to stay in the family, don't you? Mind you, they might not want to touch me in the way they wanted to touch her.

Pause.

But, Robert, you must understand that I not only want to be your wife, but also your employee. I'm not embarrassing you, am I, Willy?

WILLY. No, of course you're not.

DIANA. Because by being your employee I can help to further your interests, our interests. That's what I want to do. And so does Willy, don't you?

Disson's office. Morning.

DISSON *alone. He stands in the centre of the room. He looks at the door, walks over to* WENDY'S *desk. He looks down at her desk-chair. He touches it. Slowly, he sits in it. He sits still.*

The door opens. WENDY *comes in. He stands.*

DISSON. You're late.

WENDY. You were sitting in my chair, Mr Disson.

DISSON. I said you're late.

WENDY. I'm not at all.

    WENDY *walks to her desk.*

    DISSON *makes way for her. He moves across the room.*

I'm hurt.

DISSON. Why?

WENDY. I've put on my new dress.

    He turns, looks at her.

DISSON. When did you put it on?

WENDY. This morning.

    Pause.

DISSON. Where?

WENDY. In my flat.

DISSON. Which room?

WENDY. In the hall, actually. I have a long mirror in the hall.

    He stands looking at her.

Do you like it?

DISSON. Yes. Very nice.

Disson's house. Workroom.

DISSON. Hold it firmly. You're not holding it firmly.

> TOM *holds a length of wood on the table.* DISSON *chips at its base.*

Use pressure. Grip it.

JOHN. A clamp would be better.

DISSON. A clamp? I want you boys to learn how to concentrate your physical energies, to do something useful.

JOHN. What's it going to be, Dad?

DISSON. You'll find out.

> DISSON *chips. He straightens.*

Give me the saw.

JOHN. Me?

DISSON. The saw! Give me it! (*To* TOM.) What are you doing?

TOM. I'm holding this piece of wood.

DISSON. Well, stop it. I've finished chipping. Look at the point now.

JOHN. If you put some lead in there you could make a pencil out of it.

DISSON. They think you're very witty at your school, do they?

JOHN. Well, some do and some don't, actually, Dad.

DISSON. You. Take the saw.

TOM. Me?

DISSON. I want you to saw it off . . . from here.

> DISSON *makes a line with his finger on the wood.*

TOM. But I can't saw.

JOHN. What about our homework, Dad? We've got to write an essay about the Middle Ages.

DISSON. Never mind the Middle Ages.

JOHN. Never mind the *Middle Ages*?

TOM. Can't you demonstrate how to do it, Dad? Then we could watch.

DISSON. Oh, give me it.

DISSON *takes the saw and points to a mark on the wood.*
Now . . . from here.

TOM (*pointing*). You said from here.

DISSON. No, no, from here.

JOHN (*pointing to the other end*). I could have sworn you said
from there.

Pause.

DISSON. Go to your room.

Pause.

Get out.

JOHN *goes out.* DISSON *looks at* TOM.

Do you want to learn anything?

TOM. Yes.

DISSON. Where did I say I was going to saw it?

He stares at the wood. TOM *holds it still.*

Hold it still. Hold it. Don't let it move.

DISSON *saws. The saw is very near* TOM'S *fingers.* TOM
looks down tensely. DISSON *saws through.*

TOM. You nearly cut my fingers off.

DISSON. No, I didn't . . . I didn't . . .

He glares suddenly at TOM.

You didn't hold the wood still!

Disson's office.
The curtains are drawn.

DISSON. Come here. Put your chiffon round my eyes. My
eyes hurt.

WENDY *ties a chiffon scarf round his eyes.*

I want you to make a call to Newcastle, to Mr Martin.
We're still waiting for delivery of goods on Invoice No.
634729. What is the cause for delay?

WENDY *picks up the telephone, dials, waits.*

WENDY. Could I have Newcastle 77254, please. Thank you.
She waits. He touches her body.

Yes, I'm holding.

He touches her. She moves under his touch.

Hullo, Mr Martin, please. Mr Disson's office.

Camera on him. His arm stretching.

Mr Martin? Mr Disson's office. Mr Disson . . . Ah, you know what it's about (*She laughs.*) Yes . . . Yes.

Camera on him. He leans forward, his arm stretching.

Oh, it's been dispatched? Oh good. Mr Disson will be glad.

She moves under his touch.

Oh, I will. Of course I will.

She puts the phone down. He withdraws his hand.

Mr Martin sends his apologies. The order has been dispatched.

The intercom buzzes. She switches through. WILLY'S *voice.*

Yes?

WILLY. Oh, Wendy, is Mr Disson there?

WENDY. Did you want to speak to him, Mr Torrance?

WILLY. No. Just ask him if I might borrow your services for five minutes.

WENDY. Mr Torrance wants to know if he might borrow my services for five minutes.

DISSON. What's happened to his own secretary?

WENDY. Mr Disson would like to know what has happened to your own secretary.

WILLY. She's unwell. Gone home. Just five minutes, that's all.

DISSON *gestures towards the door.*

WENDY. Be with you in a minute, Mr Torrance.

WILLY. Please thank Mr Disson for me.

The intercom switches off.

WENDY. Mr Torrance would like me to thank you for him.

DISSON. I heard.

WENDY *goes through the inner door into* WILLY'S *office, shuts it.*

Silence.

DISSON *sits still, the chiffon round his eyes. He looks towards the door.*

He hears giggles, hissing, gurgles, squeals.

He goes to the door, squats by the handle, raises the chiffon, tries to look through the keyhole. Can see nothing through the keyhole. He drops the chiffon, puts his ear to the door. The handle presses into his skull. The sounds continue. Sudden silence.

The door has opened.

A pair of woman's legs stand by his squatting body.

He freezes, slowly puts forward a hand, touches a leg. He tears the chiffon from his eyes. It hangs from his neck. He looks up.

DIANA *looks down at him.*

Behind her, in the other room, WENDY *is sitting, taking dictation from* WILLY, *who is standing.*

DIANA. What game is this?

   He remains.

Get up. What are you doing? What are you doing with that scarf? Get up from the floor. What are you doing?

DISSON. Looking for something.

DIANA. What?

   WILLY *walks to the door, smiles, closes the door.*

What were you looking for? Get up.

DISSON (*standing*). Don't speak to me like that. How dare you speak to me like that? I'll knock your teeth out.

   She covers her face.

What were you doing in there? I thought you'd gone home. What were you doing in there?

DIANA. I came back.

DISSON. You mean you were in there with both of them? In there with both of them?

DIANA. Yes! So what?

   Pause.

DISSON (*calmly*). I was looking for my pencil, which had rolled off my desk. Here it is. I found it, just before you came in, and put it in my pocket. My eyes hurt. I borrowed Wendy's scarf, to calm my eyes. Why are you getting so excited?

Disson's office. Day.
DISSON *at his desk, writing.* WENDY *walks to the cabinet, examines a file. Silence.*

DISSON. What kind of flat do you have, Wendy?

WENDY. Quite a small one, Mr Disson. Quite pleasant.

DISSON. Not too big for you, then? Too lonely?

WENDY. Oh no, it's quite small. Quite cosy.

DISSON. Bathroom fittings any good?

WENDY. Adequate, Mr Disson. Not up to our standard.
    Pause.

DISSON. Live there alone, do you?

WENDY. No, I share it with a girl friend. But she's away quite a lot of the time. She's an air hostess. She wants me to become one, as a matter of fact.

DISSON. Listen to me, Wendy. Don't ever . . . dream of becoming an air hostess. Never. The glamour may dazzle from afar, but, believe you me, it's a mess of a life . . . a mess of a life . . .

    He watches WENDY *walk to her desk with a file and then back to the cabinet.*

Were you lonely as a child?

WENDY. No.

DISSON. Nor was I. I had quite a lot of friends. True friends. Most of them live abroad now, of course – banana planters, oil engineers, Jamaica, the Persian Gulf . . . but if I were to meet them tomorrow, you know . . . just like that . . . there'd be no strangeness, no awkwardness at all. We'd continue where we left off, quite naturally.

    WENDY *bends low at the cabinet.*
    He stares at her buttocks.

It's a matter of a core of affection, you see . . . a core of
undying affection . . .

Suddenly WENDY'S *body appears in enormous close-up. Her
buttocks fill the screen.*

His hands go up to keep them at bay.

His elbow knocks a round table lighter from his desk.

Picture normal.

WENDY *turns from the cabinet, stands upright.*

WENDY. What was that?

DISSON. My lighter.

She goes to his desk.

WENDY. Where is it?

*She kneels, looks under the desk. The lighter is at his feet.
She reaches for it. He kicks it across the room.*

(*Laughing.*) Oh, Mr Disson, why did you do that?

*She stands. He stands. She goes towards the lighter. He gets
to it before her, stands with it at his feet. He looks at her.
She stops.*

What's this?

DISSON *feints his body, left to right.*

DISSON. Come on.

WENDY. What?

DISSON. Tackle me. Get the ball.

WENDY. What do I tackle with?

DISSON. Your feet.

She moves forward deliberately.

*He dribbles away, turns, kicks the lighter along the carpet
towards her. Her foot stops the lighter. She turns with it at
her foot.*

Ah!

*She stands, legs apart, the lighter between them, staring at
him.*

She taps her foot.

WENDY. Come on, then!

He goes towards her. She eludes him. He grasps her arm.

That's a foul!

He drops her arm.

DISSON. Sorry.

She stands with the lighter between her feet.

WENDY. Come on, come on. Tackle me, tackle me. Come on, tackle me! Get the ball! Fight for the ball!

He begins to move, stops, sinks to the floor. She goes to him. What's the matter?

DISSON. Nothing. All right. Nothing.

WENDY. Let me help you up.

DISSON. No. Stay. You're very valuable in this office. Good worker. Excellent. If you have any complaints, just tell me. I'll soon put them right. You're a very efficient secretary. Something I've always needed. Have you everything you want? Are your working conditions satisfactory?

WENDY. Perfectly.

DISSON. Oh good. Good . . . Good.

Disson's house. Bedroom. Night.

DISSON *and* DIANA *in bed, reading. She looks at him.*

DIANA. You seem a little subdued . . . lately.

DISSON. Me? Not at all. I'm reading the Life of Napoleon, that's all.

DIANA. No, I don't mean now, I mean generally. Is there – ?

DISSON. I'm not at all subdued. Really.

Pause.

DIANA. It's our first anniversary next Wednesday, did you know that?

DISSON. Of course I did. How could I forget? We'll go out together in the evening. Just you and I. Alone.

DIANA. Oh. Good.

DISSON. I'm also giving a little tea party in the office, in the afternoon. My mother and father'll be up.

DIANA. Oh good.

Pause.

DISSON. How have you enjoyed our first year?

DIANA. It's been wonderful. It's been a very exciting year.
    Pause.

DISSON. You've been marvellous with the boys.

DIANA. They like me.

DISSON. Yes, they do. They do.
    Pause.

It's been a great boon, to have you work for the firm.

DIANA. Oh, I'm glad. I am glad.
    Pause.

Be nice to get away to Spain.
    Pause.

DISSON. You've got enough money, haven't you? I mean, you
    have sufficient money to see you through, for all you want?

DIANA. Oh yes. I have, thank you.
    Pause.

DISSON. I'm very proud of you, you know.

DIANA. I'm proud of you.
    Silence.

Disson's office.

DISSON. Have you written to Corley?

WENDY. Yes, Mr Disson.

DISSON. And Turnbull?

WENDY. Yes, Mr Disson.

DISSON. And Erverley?

WENDY. Yes, Mr Disson.

DISSON. Carbon of the Erverley letter, please.

WENDY. Here you are, Mr Disson.

DISSON. Ah. I see you've spelt Erverley right.

WENDY. Right?

DISSON. People tend, very easily, to leave out the first R and
    call him Everley. You haven't done that.

WENDY. No. (*She turns.*)

DISSON. Just a minute. How did you spell Turnbull? You needn't show me. Tell me.

WENDY. TURNBULL.

DISSON. Quite correct.

   Pause.

   Quite correct. Now what about – ?

      The screen goes black.

   Where are you?

      Pause.

   I can't see you.

WENDY. I'm here, Mr Disson.

DISSON. Where?

WENDY. You're looking at me, Mr Disson.

DISSON. You mean my eyes are open?

   Pause.

WENDY. I'm where I was. I haven't moved.

DISSON. Are my eyes open?

WENDY. Mr Disson, really . . .

DISSON. Is this you? This I feel?

WENDY. Yes.

DISSON. What, all this I can feel?

WENDY. You're playing one of your games, Mr Disson. You're being naughty again.

   Vision back.

   DISSON *looks at her.*

   You sly old thing.

Disley's surgery.
A torch shines in DISSON'S *eyes, first right, then left. Torch out.*
Light on.

DISLEY. There's nothing wrong with them.

DISSON. What then?

DISLEY. I only deal with eyes, old chap. Why do you come to me? Why don't you go to someone else?

DISSON. Because it's my eyes that are affected.

DISLEY. Look. Why don't you go to someone else?

DISLEY *begins to clear away his instruments.*

Nothing worrying you, is there?

DISSON. Of course not. I've got everything I want.

DISLEY. Getting a holiday soon?

DISSON. Going to Spain.

DISLEY. Lucky man.

Pause.

DISSON. Look. Listen. You're my oldest friend. You were going to be the best man at my wedding.

DISLEY. That's right.

DISSON. You wrote a wonderful speech in my honour.

DISLEY. Yes.

DISSON. But you were ill. You had to opt out.

DISLEY. That's right.

Pause.

DISSON. Help me.

Pause.

DISLEY. Who made the speech? Your brother-in-law, wasn't it?

DISSON. I don't want you to think I'm not a happy man. I am.

DISLEY. What sort of speech did he make?

Disson's house. Sitting-room. Evening.

DISSON. Tell me about Sunderley.

WILLY. Sunderley?

DISSON. Tell me about the place where you two were born. Where you played at being brother and sister.

WILLY. We didn't have to play at being brother and sister. We were brother and sister.

DIANA. Stop drinking.

DISSON. Drinking? You call this drinking? This? I used to down eleven or nine pints a night! Eleven or nine pints! Every night of the stinking week! Me and the boys! The boys! And me! I'd break any man's hand for . . . for playing me false. That was before I became a skilled craftsman. That was before . . .

> *He falls silent, sits.*

WILLY. Sunderley was beautiful.

DISSON. I know.

WILLY. And now it's gone, for ever.

DISSON. I never got there.

> DISSON *stands, goes to get a drink.*
> *He turns from drinks table.*

What are you whispering about? Do you think I don't hear? Think I don't see? I've got my memories, too. Long before this.

WILLY. Yes, Sunderley was beautiful.

DISSON. The lake.

WILLY. The lake.

DISSON. The long windows.

WILLY. From the withdrawing-room.

DISSON. On to the terrace.

WILLY. Music playing.

DISSON. On the piano.

WILLY. The summer nights. The wild swans.

DISSON. What swans? What bloody swans?

WILLY. The owls.

DISSON. Negroes at the gate, under the trees.

WILLY. No Negroes.

DISSON. Why not?

WILLY. We had no Negroes.

DISSON. Why in God's name not?

WILLY. Just one of those family quirks, Robert.

DIANA (*standing*). Robert.

> *Pause.*

Come to bed.

DISSON. You can say that, in front of him?

DIANA. Please.

DISSON. In front of *him*?

He goes to her.

Why did you marry me?

DIANA. I admired you. You were so positive.

DISSON. You loved me.

DIANA. You were kind.

DISSON. You loved me for that?

DIANA. I found you admirable in your clarity of mind, your surety of purpose, your will, the strength your achievements had given you –

DISSON. And you adored me for it?

WILLY (*to* DISSON). Can I have a private word with you?

DISSON. You *adored* me for it?

Pause.

DIANA. You know I did.

WILLY. Can I have a private word with you, old chap? (*To* DIANA.) Please.

DIANA *goes out of the room.*

DISSON *looks at* WILLY.

DISSON. Mind how you tread, Bill. Mind . . . how you tread, old Bill, old boy, old Bill.

WILLY. Listen. I've been wondering. Is there anything on your mind?

DISSON. My mind? No, of course not.

WILLY. You're not dissatisfied with my work, or anything?

DISSON. Quite the contrary. Absolutely the contrary.

WILLY. Oh good. I like the work very much. Try to do my best.

DISSON. Listen. I want you to be my partner. Hear me? I want you to share full responsibility . . . with me.

WILLY. Do you really?

DISSON. Certainly.

WILLY. Well, thank you very much. I don't know what to say.
DISSON. Don't say anything.

Disson's office.
WILLY *at the door.*
WILLY. Coming, old chap?
DISSON. Yes.
WILLY (*to* WENDY). Important lunch, this. But I think we'll swing it, don't you, Robert? (*To* WENDY.) Great prospects in store.

> DISSON *and* WILLY *go out.* WENDY *clips some papers together.*

> DIANA *comes in through the inner door.*
WENDY. Oh, hullo, Mrs Disson.
DIANA. Hullo, Wendy.

> *Pause.*

> DIANA *watches* WENDY *clip the papers.*

Do you like being a secretary?
WENDY. I do, yes. Do you?
DIANA. I do, yes.

> *Pause.*

I understand your last employer touched your body . . . rather too much.
WENDY. It wasn't a question of too much, Mrs Disson. One touch was enough for me.
DIANA. Oh, you left after the first touch?
WENDY. Well, not quite the first no.

> *Pause.*

DIANA. Have you ever asked yourself why men will persist in touching women?
WENDY. No, I've never asked myself that, Mrs Disson.
DIANA. Few women do ask themselves that question.
WENDY. Don't they? I don't know. I've never spoken to any other women on the subject.

DIANA. You're speaking to me.

WENDY. Yes. Well, have you ever asked yourself that question, Mrs Disson?

DIANA. Never. No.

Pause.

Have lunch with me today. Tell me about yourself.

WENDY. I'll have lunch with you with pleasure.

DISSON *comes in. They look at him. He at them. Silence.*

DISSON. Forgotten . . . one of the designs.

DIANA *smiles at him.* WENDY *clips her papers. He goes to his desk, collects a folder, stands upright.*

DIANA *looks out of the window.* WENDY *clips papers. He looks at them, goes out.* DIANA *and* WENDY *remain silent.*

Disson's house. Games room.

DISSON *and* WILLY *playing ping-pong. They are in the middle of a long rally.* THE TWINS *watch.* WILLY *is on the attack,* DISSON *playing desperately, retrieving from positions of great difficulty. He cuts, chops, pushes.*

TWINS (*variously*). Well done, Dad. Good shot, Dad. Good one, Dad.

WILLY *forces* DISSON *on to the forehand. He slams viciously.* DISSON *skids.*

The screen goes black.

Good shot!

DISSON. Aaah!

Vision back.

DISSON *is clutching the table, bent over it.*

WILLY *throws the ball on to the table.*

It bounces gently across it.

Disson's house. Sitting-room. Evening.

DISSON'S *parents.*

MOTHER. Have I seen that mirror before?

DISSON. No. It's new.

MOTHER. I knew I hadn't seen it. Look at it, John. What a beautiful mirror.

FATHER. Must have cost you a few bob.

MOTHER. Can you see the work on it. John? I bet it must be a few years old, that mirror.

DISSON. It's a few hundred years old.

FATHER. I bet it must have cost you a few bob.

DISSON. It wasn't cheap.

FATHER. Cheap?

MOTHER. What a beautiful mirror.

FATHER. Cheap? Did you hear what he said, Dora? He said it wasn't cheap!

MOTHER. No, I bet it wasn't.

FATHER (*laughing*). Cheap!

    Pause.

MOTHER. Mrs Tidy sends you her love.

DISSON. Who?

FATHER. Mrs Tidy. The Tidys.

DISSON. Oh yes. How are they?

FATHER. Still very tidy. (*Laughs.*) Aren't they, Dora?

MOTHER. You remember the Tidys.

DISSON. Of course I remember them.

    Pause.

How have you been keeping, then?

FATHER. Oh, your mother's had a few pains. You know, just a few.

MOTHER. Only a few, John. I haven't had many pains.

FATHER. I only said you'd had a few. Not many.

    Pause.

MOTHER. Are the boys looking forward to their holiday?

DISSON. Yes, they are.

FATHER. When are you going?

DISSON. I'm not.

Disson's office.

DISSON. Tighter.

   WENDY *ties the chiffon round his eyes.*

WENDY. There. You look nice.

DISSON. This chiffon stinks.

WENDY. Oh, I do apologize. What of?

   Pause.

You're very rude to me. But you do look nice. You really do.

   DISSON *tears the chiffon off.*

DISSON. It's useless. Ring Disley. Tell him to come here.

WENDY. But he'll be here at four o'clock, for your tea party.

DISSON. I want him now! I want him . . . now.

WENDY. Don't you like my chiffon any more, to put round
your eyes? My lovely chiffon?

   Pause.

   He sits still.

I always feel like kissing you when you've got that on round
your eyes. Do you know that? Because you're all in the dark.

   Pause.

Put it on.

   She picks up the chiffon and folds it.

I'll put it on . . . for you. Very gently.

   She leans forward.

   He touches her.

No -- you mustn't touch me, if you're not wearing your
chiffon.

   She places the chiffon on his eyes.

   *He trembles, puts his hand to the chiffon, slowly lowers it,
lets it fall.*

   It flutters to the floor.

   As she looks at him, he reaches for the telephone.

Disson's office.

DISSON *in the same position.*

DISSON. I need a tight bandage. Very tight.

DISLEY. Anyone could do that for you.

DISSON. No. You're my eye consultant. You must do it for me.

DISLEY. All right.

> *He takes a bandage from his case and ties it round* DISSON'S *eyes.*

Just for half an hour. You don't want it on when your guests arrive, do you?

> DISLEY *ties the knots.*

This'll keep you in the dark, all right. Also lend pressure to your temples. Is that what you want?

DISSON. That's it. That's what I want.

> DISLEY *cuts the strands.*

DISLEY. There. How's that?

> *Pause.*

See anything?

Disson's office. Afternoon.

DISSON *sits alone, the bandage round his eyes.*

Silence.

WILLY *enters from his office. He sees* DISSON *and goes to him.*

WILLY. How are you, old chap? Bandage on straight? Knots tight?

> *He pats him on the back and goes out through the front office door.*
> *The door slams.*
> DISSON *sits still.*

Corridor.

MR *and* MRS DISLEY *approaching the office.*

LOIS. Why didn't he make it a cocktail party? Why a tea party, of all things?
DISLEY. I couldn't say.

Office.
DISSON'S *head.*
Soft clicks of door opening and closing, muffled steps, an odd cough, slight rattle of teacups.

Corridor.
DISSON'S *parents approaching the office.*
MOTHER. I could do with a cup of tea, couldn't you, John?

Office.
DISSON'S *head.*
Soft clicks of door opening and closing, muffled steps, an odd cough, slight rattle of teacups.

Corridor.
THE TWINS *approach, silent.*

Office.
DISSON'S *head.*
Soft clicks of door opening and closing, muffled steps, an odd cough, slight rattle of teacups, a short whisper.

Corridor.
DIANA *and* WILLY *approach.*
DIANA. Why *don't* you come to Spain with us?
WILLY. I think I will.

Office.
DISSON'S *head.*
Soft clicks of door opening and closing, muffled steps, an odd cough,
   slight rattle of teacups, whispers.

Corridor.
WENDY *approaches.*

Office.
DISSON'S *head.*
Soft clicks of door opening and closing, muffled steps, an odd cough,
slight rattle of teacups, whispers.

Office.
A buffet table has been set out. Two ELDERLY LADIES *serve*
tea, sandwiches, bridge rolls, buns and cakes. The gathering is
grouped around the table in silence. DISLEY *whispers to them.*
DISLEY. His eyes are a little strained, that's all. Just resting
   them a little. Don't mention it. It'll embarrass him. It's
   quite all right.
      They all take their tea, choose edibles, and relax.
JOHN (*choosing a cake*). These are good.
TOM. What are they?
DIANA (*choosing a bridge roll*). These look nice.
LOIS. You look wonderful, Mrs Disson. Absolutely wonderful.
   Doesn't she, Peter?
DISLEY. Marvellous.
LOIS. What do you think of your grandsons?
FATHER. They've grown up now, haven't they?

LOIS. Of course, we knew them when they were that high, didn't we, Tom?

FATHER. So did we.

TOM. Yes.

WILLY. Big lads now, aren't they, these two?

JOHN. Cake, Granny?

MOTHER. No, I've had one.

JOHN. Have two.

FATHER. I'll have one.

MOTHER. He's had one.

FATHER. I'll have two.

> WENDY *takes a cup of tea to* DISSON *and puts it into his hands.*

WENDY. Here's a cup of tea, Mr Disson. Drink it. It's warm.

LOIS (*to* DIANA). You're off to Spain quite soon, aren't you, Diana?

DIANA. Yes, quite soon.

DISLEY (*calling*). We'll take off those bandages in a minute, old chap!

LOIS. Spain is wonderful at this time of the year.

WILLY. Any time of the year, really.

LOIS. But I think it's best at this time of the year, don't you?

DIANA. What sun lotion do you use, Lois?

DISSON'S *point of view.*
No dialogue is heard in all shots from DISSON'S *point of view.*
Silence.
Figures mouthing silently, in conspiratorial postures, seemingly whispering together.

Shot including DISSON.

TOM. I went into goal yesterday.

WILLY. How did you do?

LOIS. You can get it anywhere. It's perfect.

JOHN. He made two terrific saves.

TOM. The first was a fluke.

LOIS. How do you sun, then?

DIANA. I have to be rather careful.

TOM. Second save wasn't a bad save.

LOIS. How do you sun, Wendy?

WENDY. Oh, not too bad, really.

LOIS (*to* MRS DISSON). We go to our little island every year and when we go we have to leave our poor little Siamese with my mother.

MOTHER. Do you really?

LOIS. They're almost human, aren't they, Siamese?

DIANA. I'm sure my Siamese was.

LOIS. Aren't they, Peter, almost human?

DIANA. Wasn't Tiger a human cat, Willy, at Sunderley?

WILLY. He adored you.

DISLEY. They really are almost human, aren't they, Siamese?

DISSON'S *point of view.*
Silence.
The party splits into groups. Each group whispering.
The two ELDERLY LADIES *at the buffet table.*
DISSON'S PARENTS, *sitting together.*
THE TWINS *and the* DISLEYS.
WILLY, WENDY *and* DIANA *in a corner.*

Shot including DISSON.
The gathering in a close group, the PARENTS *sitting.*
LOIS. I'd go like a shot.

WENDY. What, me? Come to Spain?

DIANA. Yes, why not?

    WILLY *leans across* DISLEY.

WILLY. Yes, of course you must come. Of course you must come.

WENDY. How wonderful.

DISSON'S *point of view.*
WILLY *approaches* DISSON. *With a smile, he takes a ping-pong ball from his pocket, and puts it into* DISSON'S *hand.*
DISSON *clutches it.*

DISSON'S *point of view.*
WILLY *returns to* WENDY *and* DIANA, *whispers to them.*
DIANA *laughs (silently), head thrown back, gasps with laughter.*
WENDY *smiles.*
WILLY *puts one arm round* WENDY, *the other round* DIANA.
He leads them to WENDY'S *desk.*
WILLY *places cushions on the desk.*
DIANA *and* WENDY, *giggling silently, hoist themselves up on to the desk. They lie head to toe.*

DISSON'S *point of view. Close-up.*
WENDY'S *face.* WILLY'S *fingers caressing it.* DIANA'S *shoes in background.*

DISSON'S *point of view. Close-up.*
DIANA'S *face.* WILLY'S *fingers caressing it.* WENDY'S *shoes in background.*

DISSON'S *point of view.*
LOIS *powdering her nose.*

DISSON'S *point of view.*
The ELDERLY LADIES *drinking tea, at the table.*

DISSON'S *point of view.*
DISLEY *talking to the boys by the window.* THE TWINS *listening intently.*

DISSON'S *point of view.*
DISSON'S PARENTS *sitting, dozing.*

DISSON'S *point of view.*
The base of WENDY'S *desk.*
A shoe drops to the floor.

Shot including DISSON.
DISSON *falls to the floor in his chair with a crack. His teacup drops and spills.*
The gathering is grouped by the table, turns.
DISLEY *and* WILLY *go to him.*
They try to lift him from the chair, are unable to do so.
DISLEY *cuts the bandage and takes it off.*
DISSON'S *eyes are open.*
DISLEY *feels his pulse.*
DISLEY. He's all right. Get him up.

> DISLEY *and* WILLY *try to pull him up from the chair, are unable to do so.*
>
> JOHN *and* TOM *join them.*

Get it up.

The four of them, with great effort, manage to set the chair on its feet.

DISSON is still seated.

He must lie down. Now, two hold the chair, and two pull him.

JOHN and WILLY hold the chair.

DISLEY and TOM pull.

The chair.

The chair scrapes, moves no further.

The group around the chair.

They pull, with great effort.

The chair.

The chair scrapes, moves no further.

The room.

WILLY. Anyone would think he was chained to it!

DISLEY (*pulling*). Come out!

MOTHER. Bobbie!

They stop pulling.

DISSON in the chair, still, his eyes open.

DIANA comes to him.

She kneels by him.

DIANA. This is . . . Diana.

Pause.

Can you hear me?

Pause.

Can he see me?

Pause.

Robert.
  Pause.
Can you hear me?
  Pause.
Robert, can you see me?
  Pause.
It's me. It's me, darling.
  Slight pause.
It's your wife.

DISSON'S *face in close-up.*
  DISSON'S *eyes. Open.*

THE BASEMENT

THE BASEMENT was first presented by B.B.C. Television on
1967 with the following cast:

STOTT   Harold Pinter

JANE   Kika Markham

LAW   Derek Godfrey

Directed by Charles Jarrott

Exterior. Front area of a basement flat.
Winter. Night.
Rain falling.
Short stone flight of steps from street.
Light shining through the basement door.
The upper part of the house is dark.
The back of a man, STOTT. *He stands in the centre of the area,*
looking towards the door.
He wears a raincoat, his head is bare.

Exterior. Front area.
STOTT'S *face. Behind him, by the wall, a girl,* JANE. *She is*
huddled by the wall. She wears a rainhat, clasps her raincoat to
her.

Interior. Room.
The room is large and long. A window at one end looks out to a
small concrete yard. There are doors to bathroom and kitchen.
The room is comfortable, relaxed, heavily furnished.
Numerous side tables, plants, arm-chairs, book-cabinets, book-
shelves, velvet cloths, a desk, paintings, a large double bed. There
is a large fire in the grate.
The room is lit by a number of table and standard lamps.
LAW *is lying low in an arm-chair, reading, by the fireside.*
Silence.

Exterior. Front area.
STOTT *still.*

Interior. Room.
LAW *in arm-chair. He is smiling at his book.*
He giggles. He is reading a Persian love manual, with illustrations.

Exterior. Front area.
JANE *huddled by the wall.*
STOTT *moves to the door.*

Interior. Room.
Doorbell. LAW *looks up from his book. He closes it, puts it on a side table, goes into the hall.*

Interior. Small hall.
LAW *approaches the front door. He opens it.*
Silence.
He stares at STOTT. *From his position in the doorway* LAW *cannot see the girl.*
LAW (*with great pleasure*). Stott!
STOTT (*smiling*). Hullo, Tim.
LAW. Good God. Come in!

LAW *laughs.*
Come in!
STOTT *enters.*
I can't believe it!

Interior. Room.
LAW *and* STOTT *enter.*
LAW. Give me your coat. You're soaking. Come on. That's it. I'm absolutely flabbergasted. You must be freezing.
STOTT. I am a bit.
LAW. Go on, warm yourself. Warm yourself by the fire.

STOTT. Thanks.

LAW. Sit down by the fire. Go on.

> STOTT *moves to the fire.*
> LAW *takes the coat into hall.*

Interior. Hall.

LAW *comes into the hall, shaking the raincoat. He looks inside it, at the label, smiles. He hangs it on a hook.*

Interior. Room.

STOTT *warming his hands at the fire.* LAW *comes in.*

LAW. You haven't changed at all. You haven't changed . . . at all!

> STOTT *laughs.*

You've got a new raincoat though. Oh yes, I noticed. Hold on, I'll get you a towel.

> LAW *goes to the bathroom.*
> STOTT, *alone, looks up and about him at the room.*

Interior. Room.
The room.

Interior. Bathroom.

LAW *in bathroom, at the airing cupboard. He swiftly throws aside a number of towels, chooses a soft one with a floral pattern.*

Interior. Room.

LAW *comes in with a towel.*

LAW. Here's a towel. Go on, give it a good wipe. That's it.

You didn't walk here, did you? You're soaking. What happened to your car? You could have driven here. Why didn't you give me a ring? But how did you know my address? My God, it's years. If you'd have rung I would have picked you up. I would have picked you up in my car. What happened to your car?

   STOTT *finishes drying his hair, puts the towel on the arm of a chair.*

STOTT. I got rid of it.

LAW. But how are you? Are you well? You look well.

STOTT. How are you?

LAW. Oh, I'm well. Just a minute, I'll get you some slippers.
   LAW *goes to the cupboard, bends.*

You're going to stay the night, aren't you? You'll have to, look at the time. I wondered if you'd ever turn up again. Really. For years. Here you are. Here's some slippers.

STOTT. Thanks.

   STOTT *takes the slippers, changes his shoes.*

LAW. I'll find some pyjamas in a minute. Still, we'll have a cup of coffee first, or some . . . Or a drink? What about a drink?

STOTT. Ah.

   LAW *pours drinks, brings the drinks to the sofa and sits down by* STOTT.

LAW. You're not living at Chatsworth Road any more, are you? I know that. I've passed by there, numbers of times. You've moved. Where are you living now?

STOTT. I'm looking for a place.

LAW. Stay here! Stay here as long as you like. I've got another bed I can fit up. I've got a camp bed I can fit up.

STOTT. I don't want to impose upon you.

LAW. Not a bit, not a bit.

   Pause.

STOTT. Oh, by the way, I've got a friend outside. Can she come in?

LAW. A friend?

STOTT. Outside.

LAW. A friend? Outside?

STOTT. Can she come in?

LAW. Come in? Yes . . . yes . . . of course . . .

    STOTT *goes towards the door.*

  What's she doing outside?

Exterior. Front door.
JANE *is standing in the narrow porch outside the door.*
The door opens.

Interior. Room.
LAW. STOTT *brings the girl in.*

STOTT. This is Jane. This is Tim Law.

    She smiles.

JANE. It's kind of you.

LAW. How do you do? I . . . must get you a towel.

JANE. No, thank you. My hair was covered.

LAW. But your face?

    STOTT *comes forward.*

STOTT. It's very kind of you, Tim. It really is. Here's a towel.
  (*He gives it to her.*) Here.

LAW. But that's your towel.

JANE. I don't mind, really.

LAW. I have clean ones, dry ones.

JANE (*patting her face*). This is clean.

LAW. But it's not dry.

JANE. It's very soft.

LAW. I have others.

JANE. There. I'm dry.

LAW. You can't be.

JANE. What a splendid room.

STOTT. Isn't it? A little bright, perhaps.

LAW. Too much light?

> STOTT *turns a lamp off.*

STOTT. Do you mind?

LAW. No.

> JANE *begins to take her clothes off.*
> *In the background* STOTT *moves about the room, turning off the lamps.*
> LAW *stands still.*
> STOTT *turns off all the lamps but one, by the fireside.*
> JANE, *naked, gets into the bed.*

Can I get you some cocoa? Some hot chocolate?

> STOTT *takes his clothes off and, naked, gets into the bed.*

I was feeling quite lonely, actually. It is lonely sitting here, night after night. Mind you, I'm very happy here. Remember that place we shared? That awful place in Chatsworth Road? I've come a long way since then. I bought this flat cash down. It's mine. I don't suppose you've noticed the hi-fi stereo? There's all sorts of things I can show you.

> LAW *unbuttons his cardigan.*
> *He places it over the one lit lamp, so shading the light. He sits by the fire.*

The lamp covered by the cardigan.

Patch of light on the ceiling.

Patch of light at LAW'S *feet.*

LAW'S *hands on the chair arms.*
A gasp from JANE.
LAW'S *hands do not move.*

LAW'S *legs. Beyond them, the fire almost dead.*

LAW *puts on his glasses.*

LAW *reaches for* The Persian Manual of Love.

LAW *peers to read.*
A long sigh from JANE.
LAW *reads.*

Exterior. Cliff-top. Day. Summer.
Long-shot of STOTT *standing on a cliff-top.*

Exterior. Beach.
The beach is long and deserted. LAW *and* JANE, *in swimming*
costumes. JANE *building a sandcastle.* LAW *watches her.*
LAW. How old are you?
JANE. I'm very young.
LAW. You are young.
     He watches her work.
   You're a child.
     He watches her.
   Have you known him long?
JANE. No.
LAW. I have. Charming man. Man of great gifts. Very old
   friend of mine, as a matter of fact. Has he told you?
JANE. No.
LAW. You don't know him very well?

JANE. No.

LAW. He has a connexion with the French aristocracy. He was educated in France. Speaks French fluently, of course. Have you read his French translations?

JANE. No.

LAW. Ah. They're immaculate. Great distinction. Formidable scholar, Stott. Do you know what he got at Oxford? He got a First in Sanskrit at Oxford. A First in Sanskrit!

JANE. How wonderful.

LAW. You never knew?

JANE. Never.

LAW. I know for a fact he owns three châteaux. Three superb châteaux. Have you ever ridden in his Alvis? His Facel Vega? What an immaculate driver. Have you seen his yachts? Huh! What yachts. What yachts.

> JANE *completes her sandcastle.*

How pleased I was to see him. After so long. One loses touch . . . so easily.

Interior. Cave. Day.

STOTT'S *body lying in the sand, asleep.*

LAW *and* JANE *appear at the mouth of the cave. They arrive at the body, look down.*

LAW. What repose he has.

STOTT'S *body in the sand.*

Their shadows across him.

Interior. Room. Night.

LAW *lying on the floor, a cushion at his head, covered by a blanket. His eyes are closed.*

Silence.

A long gasp from JANE.

LAW'S *eyes open.*

STOTT *and* JANE *in bed.*
STOTT *turning to the wall.*
JANE *turns to the edge of the bed.*
She leans over the edge of the bed and smiles at LAW.

LAW *looks at her.*

JANE *smiles.*

Interior. Room. Day.
STOTT *lifts a painting from the wall, looks at it.*
STOTT. No.
LAW. No, you're quite right. I've never liked it.

> STOTT *walks across room to a second picture, looks at it. He*
> *turns to look at* LAW.

No.

> STOTT *takes it down and turns to look at the other paintings.*
All of them. All of them. You're right. They're terrible. Take
them down.

> *The paintings are all similar watercolours.*
> STOTT *begins to take them from the walls.*

Interior. Kitchen. Day.
JANE *in the kitchen, cooking at the stove, humming.*

Exterior. Backyard. Winter. Day.
The yard is surrounded by high blank walls.

STOTT *and* LAW *sitting at an iron table, with a pole for an umbrella.*

They are drinking lager.

LAW. Who is she? Where did you meet her?

STOTT. She's charming, isn't she?

LAW. Charming. A little young.

STOTT. She comes from a rather splendid family, actually.

LAW. Really?

STOTT. Rather splendid.

> *Pause.*

LAW. Very helpful, of course, around the house.

STOTT. Plays the harp, you know.

LAW. Well?

STOTT. Remarkably well.

LAW. What a pity I don't possess one. You don't possess a harp, do you?

STOTT. Of course I possess a harp.

LAW. A recent acquisition?

STOTT. No, I've had it for years.

> *Pause.*

LAW. You don't find she's lacking in maturity?

Exterior. Beach. Summer. Day.

LAW *and* JANE *lying in the sand.* JANE *caressing him.*

JANE (*whispering*). Yes, yes, yes, oh you are, oh you are, oh you are . . .

LAW. We can be seen.

JANE. Why do you resist? How can you resist?

LAW. We can be seen! Damn you!

Exterior. Backyard. Winter. Day.

STOTT *and* LAW *at the table with lager.*

JANE *comes to the back door.*

JANE. Lunch is up!

Interior. Hall. Day.
LAW *and* JANE *come in at the front door with towels over their shoulders.*

Interior. Room. Day. Summer.
LAW *and* JANE *at the entrance of the room, towels over their shoulders, staring at the room.*
The room is unrecognizable. The furnishing has changed. There are Scandinavian tables and desks. Large bowls of Swedish glass. Tubular chairs. An Indian rug. Parquet floors, shining. A new hi-fi cabinet, etc. Fireplace blocked. The bed is the same.
STOTT *is at the window, closing the curtains. He turns.*
STOTT. Have a good swim?

Interior. Room. Night. Winter. (Second furnishing.)
STOTT *and* JANE *in bed, smoking.* LAW *sitting.*
STOTT. Let's have some music. We haven't heard your hi-fi for ages. Let's hear your stereo. What are you going to play?

Interior. Bar. Evening.
Large empty bar. All the tables unoccupied.
STOTT, LAW *and* JANE *at one table.*
STOTT. This was one of our old haunts, wasn't it, Tim? This was one of our haunts. Tim was always my greatest friend, you know. Always. It's marvellous. I've found my old friend again –
Looking at JANE.
And discovered a new. And you like each other so much It's really very warming.
LAW. Same again? (*To* WAITER.) Same again. (*To* JANE.

Same again? (*To* WAITER.) Same again. The same again, all round. Exactly the same.

STOTT. I'll change to Campari.

LAW (*clicking his fingers at the* WAITER). One Campari here. Otherwise the same again.

STOTT. Remember those nights reading Proust? Remember them?

LAW (*to* JANE). In the original.

STOTT. The bouts with Laforgue? What bouts.

LAW. I remember.

STOTT. The great elms they had then. The great elm trees.

LAW. And the poplars.

STOTT. The cricket. The squash courts. You were pretty hot stuff at squash, you know.

LAW. You were unbeatable.

STOTT. Your style was deceptive.

LAW. It still is.

> LAW *laughs.*

It still is!

STOTT. Not any longer.

> *The* WAITER *serves the drinks.*
>
> *Silence.* STOTT *lifts his glass.*

Yes, I really am a happy man.

Exterior. Field. Evening. Winter.

STOTT *and* LAW. JANE *one hundred yards across the field. She holds a scarf.*

LAW (*shouting*). Hold the scarf up. When you drop it, we run.

> *She holds the scarf up.*
>
> LAW *rubs his hands.* STOTT *looks at him.*

STOTT. Are you quite sure you want to do this?

LAW. Of course I'm sure.

JANE. On your marks!

> STOTT *and* LAW *get on their marks.*

Get set!
>*They get set.*
>JANE *drops scarf.*

Go!
>LAW *runs.* STOTT *stays still.*
>LAW, *going fast, turns to look for* STOTT; *off balance, stumbles, falls, hits his chin on the ground.*
>*Lying flat, he looks back at* STOTT.

LAW. Why didn't you run?

Exterior. Field.
JANE *stands, scarf in her hand. Downfield,* STOTT *stands.*
LAW *lies on the grass.* LAW'S *voice:*
LAW. Why didn't you run?

Interior. Room. Night. Winter. (Second furnishing.)
STOTT. Let's have some music. We haven't heard your hi-fi
>for ages.

>STOTT *opens the curtains and the window.*
>*Moonlight.* LAW *and* JANE *sit in chairs, clench their bodies with cold.*

Exterior. Backyard. Day. Winter.
STOTT *walking.* LAW, *wearing a heavy overcoat, collar turned up, watching him.* LAW *approaches him.*

LAW. Listen. Listen. I must speak to you. I must speak
>frankly. Listen. Don't you think it's a bit crowded in that
>flat, for the three of us?

STOTT. No, no. Not at all.

LAW. Listen, listen. Stop walking. Stop walking. Please. Wait.
>STOTT *stops.*

Listen. Wouldn't you say that the flat is a little small, for three people?

STOTT (*patting his shoulder*). No, no. Not at all.

    STOTT *continues walking.*

LAW (*following him*). To look at it another way, to look at it another way, I can assure you that the Council would object strenuously to three people living in these conditions. The Town Council, I know for a fact, would feel it incumbent upon itself to register the strongest possible objections. And so would the Church.

    STOTT *stops walking, looks at him.*

STOTT. Not at all. Not at all.

Interior. Room. Day. Summer.
The curtains are closed. The three at lunch, at the table. STOTT *and* JANE *are wearing tropical clothes.* JANE *is sitting on* STOTT'S *lap.*

LAW. Why don't we open the curtains?

    STOTT *eats a grape.*

It's terribly close. Shall I open the window?

STOTT. What are you going to play? Debussy, I hope.

    LAW *goes to the record cabinet. He examines record after record, feverishly, flings them one after the other at the wall.*

STOTT. Where's Debussy?

    STOTT *kisses* JANE.

    Another record hits the wall.

Where's Debussy? That's what we want. That's what we need. That's what we need at the moment.

    JANE *breaks away from* STOTT *and goes out into the yard.*
    STOTT *sits still.*

LAW. I've found it!

Interior. Room. Night. Winter.
LAW *turns with the record.*

The room is furnished as at the beginning.
STOTT *and* JANE, *naked, climb into bed.*
LAW *puts the record down and places his cardigan over the
one lit lamp.*
He sits, picks up the poker and pokes the dying fire.

Exterior. Backyard. Day. Summer.
JANE *sitting at the iron table.*
STOTT *approaches her with a glass and bottle.*
He pours wine into the glass.
He bends over her, attempts to touch her breast.
She moves her body away from him.
STOTT *remains still.*

LAW *watches from the open windows.*
He moves to the table with the record and smiles at STOTT.
LAW. I've found the record. The music you wanted.
> STOTT *slams his glass on the table and goes into the room.*
> LAW *sits at the table, drinks from the bottle, regards* JANE.
> JANE *plays with a curl in her hair.*

Interior. Cave by the sea. Evening. Summer.
LAW *and* JANE. *He lying, she sitting, by him.*
She bends and whispers to him.
JANE. Why don't you tell him to go? We had such a lovely
home. We had such a cosy home. It was so warm. Tell him
to go. It's your place. Then we could be happy again. Like
we used to. Like we used to. In our first blush of love. Then
we could be happy again, like we used to. We could be happy
again. Like we used to.

Exterior. Backyard. Night. Winter.
The yard is icy. The window is open. The room is lit.
LAW *is whispering to* STOTT *at the window. In the background*
JANE *sits sewing.* (*Second furnishing.*)

Exterior. Backyard. Window.
LAW *and* STOTT *at the open window,* STOTT'S *body hunched.*
LAW (*whispering very deliberately*). She betrays you. She betrays
   you. She has no loyalty. After all you've done for her. Shown
   her the world. Given her faith. You've been deluded. She's
   a savage. A viper. She sullies this room. She dirties this
   room. All this beautiful furniture. This beautiful Scandinavian furniture. She dirties it. She sullies the room.
   STOTT *turns slowly to regard* JANE.

Interior. Room. Day.
The curtains are closed.
STOTT *in bed.* JANE *bending over him, touching his head.*
She looks across at LAW.
Silence. (*Second furnishing.*)
LAW. Is he breathing?
JANE. Just.
LAW. His last, do you think?
   Pause.
   Do you think it could be his last?
JANE. It could be.
LAW. How could it have happened? He seemed so fit. He was
   fit. As fit as a fiddle. Perhaps we should have called a doctor.
   And now he's dying. Are you heartbroken?
JANE. Yes.
LAW. So am I.
   Pause.
JANE. What shall we do with the body?

LAW. Body? He's not dead yet. Perhaps he'll recover.

They stare at each other.

Interior. Room. Night.
LAW *and* JANE *in a corner, snuffling each other like animals.*

Interior. Room. Night.
STOTT *at the window. He opens the curtains. Moonlight pierces the room. He looks round.*

Interior. Room. Night.
LAW *and* JANE *in a corner, looking up at the window, blinking.*

Interior. Room. Day.
STOTT *at the window, closing the curtains. He turns into the room. The room is unrecognizable. The walls are hung with tapestries, an oval Florentine mirror, an oblong Italian Master. The floor is marble tiles. There are marble pillars with hanging plants, carved golden chairs, a rich carpet along the room's centre.*
STOTT *sits in a chair.* JANE *comes forward with a bowl of fruit.*
STOTT *chooses a grape. In the background* LAW, *in a corner, playing the flute.* STOTT *bites into the grape, tosses the bowl of fruit across the room. The fruit scatters.* JANE *rushes to collect it.*
STOTT *picks up a tray containing large marbles.*
He rolls the tray. The marbles knock against each other.
He selects a marble. He looks across the room at LAW *playing the flute.*

LAW *with flute.*
At the other end of the room STOTT *prepares to bow .*
STOTT. Play!

STOTT *bowls.*

The marble crashes into the wall behind LAW.

LAW *stands, takes guard with his flute.*

STOTT. Play!
    STOTT *bowls.*

The marble crashes into the window behind LAW.

LAW *takes guard.*
STOTT. Play!
    STOTT *bowls. The marble hits* LAW *on the knee.*

LAW *hops.*

LAW *takes guard.*

STOTT. Play!
    STOTT *bowls.*

LAW *brilliantly cuts marble straight into golden fish tank. The tank smashes. Dozens of fish swim across the marble tiles.*

JANE, *in the corner, applauds.*

LAW *waves his flute in acknowledgement.*

STOTT. Play!
    STOTT *bowls.*

Marble crashes into LAW'S *forehead. He drops.*

Interior. Kitchen. Night.
JANE *in the kitchen, putting spoonfuls of instant coffee into two cups.*

Interior. Room. Night.
The room is completely bare.
Bare walls. Bare floorboards. No furniture. One hanging bulb.
STOTT *and* LAW *at opposite ends of the room.*
They face each other. They are barefooted. They each hold a broken milk bottle. They are crouched, still.

LAW'S *face, sweating.*

STOTT'S *face, sweating.*

LAW *from* STOTT'S *viewpoint.*

STOTT *from* LAW'S *viewpoint.*

JANE *pouring sugar from a packet into the bowl.*

LAW *pointing his bottle before him, his arm taut.*

STOTT *pointing his bottle before him, his arm taut.*

JANE *pouring milk from a bottle into a jug.*

STOTT *slowly advancing along bare boards.*

LAW *slowly advancing.*

JANE *pouring a small measure of milk into the cups.*

LAW *and* STOTT *drawing closer.*

JANE *putting sugar into the cups.*

The broken milk bottles, in shaking hands, almost touching.

The broken milk bottles fencing, not touching.

JANE *stirring milk, sugar and coffee in the cups.*

The broken milk bottles, in a sudden thrust, smashing together.

Record turning on a turntable. Sudden music.
Debussy's 'Girl With The Flaxen Hair'.

Exterior. Front area. Night.
LAW *standing centre, looking at the basement door.*
JANE *crouched by the wall. Rainhat. Raincoat.* LAW *wearing*
STOTT'S *raincoat.*

Interior. Room.
Furnished as at the beginning.
STOTT *sitting by the fire, reading. He is smiling at his book.*

Exterior. Front area.
LAW *still.*

Interior. Room.
STOTT *turns a page.*
Doorbell.
STOTT *looks up, puts his book down, stands, goes into the hall.*

Interior. Room.
The room still. The fire burning.

Interior. Hall.
STOTT *approaches the front door. He opens it.*
Silence.
He stares at LAW. *From his position in the doorway*
STOTT *cannot see* JANE.
STOTT (*with great pleasure*). Law!
LAW (*smiling*). Hullo, Charles.
STOTT. Good God. Come in!

    STOTT *laughs.*

  Come in!

    LAW *enters.*

  I can't believe it!